AF470649

Looking at Pictures

Looking at Pictures

An Introduction to the Appreciation of Art

John Armstrong

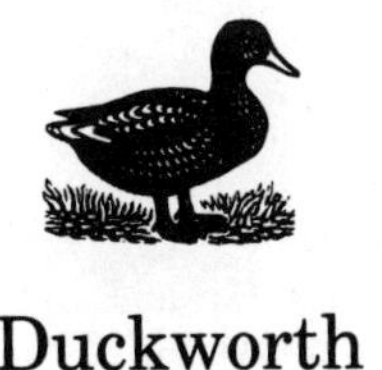

Duckworth

First published in 1996 by
Gerald Duckworth & Co. Ltd.
The Old Piano Factory
48 Hoxton Square, London N1 6PB
Tel: 0171 729 5986
Fax: 0171 729 0015

© 1996 by John Armstrong

All rights reserved. No part of this publication
may be reproduced, stored in a retrieval system, or
transmitted, in any form or by any means, electronic,
mechanical, photocopying, recording or otherwise,
without the prior permission of the publisher.

A catalogue record for this book is available
from the British Library

ISBN 0 7156 2701 5

Picture credits

The author and publisher are grateful to the following for
supplying and giving permission to reproduce illustrations:

Plates 1, 2, 3, 5, 6, 7, 8, 13, 16, 19, 22: reproduced by
    courtesy of the Trustees, The National Gallery, London
Plates 4, 10, 11, 12: Louvre, Paris; Photos RMN
Plate 9: reproduced by permission of the Trustees of
    Dulwich Picture Gallery, London
Plates 14, 18: reproduced by permission of the Trustees of
    the British Museum, London
Plate 15: Ashmolean Museum, Oxford
Plates 17, 21: Photos courtesy of the Mansell Collection,
    London
Plate 20: Courtauld Institute Galleries, London

Typeset by Ray Davies
Printed in Great Britain by
Redwood Books Ltd, Trowbridge

Contents

To Helen Hayward

List of Plates

between pages 64 and 65

From a Philosophical Point of View

This book is an introduction to looking at and thinking about paintings; it aims to enhance appreciation and to cultivate a philosophical view of art; each requires the other.

There are no shallow-ends in philosophy, wise people say. There is a certain truth in this swimming-pool analogy. You cannot do philosophy unless you take both your feet off the bottom at once: that is difficult but exhilarating; you cannot learn to swim by paddling, no matter what a dash you cut in your swimming costume. But there are deep-ends and deep-ends. Some books insist that you leap from storm-lashed rocks into raging torrents from which no one has emerged alive (Nietzsche), some take you far out to sea in a tiny, minimal skiff which then disintegrates leaving you to slip deep into the icy waters (Kant). But there are other, less traumatising deep-ends. There is the quiet, sunny pool, with clear water, calm voices and sensible help at hand; this book is, I hope, of the last kind. It is written for those who think they *might* like to do a little philosophical swimming, if the weather turns out nice. It is not a training session for Olympic racers or cross-channel champions.

This portrait of painting is drawn from a philosophical point of view. But what is it exactly to adopt a philosophical point of view? And why should one bother to do so? What can be seen from there?

Paintings, and the practices which surround painting, have generated an immense quantity of talk and of written reflection; there exists a great hinterland of thought about paintings, about their meaning and value, about our responses and about the people who paint them.

It is through our thoughts that we engage with paintings. Our collection (and each individual's collection) of habitual thoughts and patterns of thought is like a tool-kit. Thoughts are instruments we employ when we engage with the world; the quality of that engagement depends in large part upon the suitability of the tools for the task and upon their condition. Is one using a pair of scissors to cut the grass or, if one is using a lawn-mower, have the blades been sharpened recently?

There can be ways in which our thoughts and patterns of thought actually prevent us from engaging intimately with paintings. The predominant way in which this happens is through using unsuitable tools for the task in hand. Paintings are sensitive, delicate and complex things. If our conceptual tool-kit consists (as it were) only of a rusty saw and a broken hammer, it is going to be a messy business when we get to close quarters with painting.

Philosophy is the humane discipline of servicing our intellectual tool-kit and of assessing the adequacy of the tools to the current business. Philosophy is the hand-maiden of thinking. To view painting from a philosophical point of view, then, is to consider the ideas, thoughts and notions which we make use of when we look at and reflect upon paintings; this is done with the aim of developing the quality of our engagement with paintings. The sovereign question might be put thus: How do we need to think about paintings if we are to appreciate them?

There are basically three resources which philosophy has to offer the thinker: conceptual analysis, the logical evaluation of arguments, and the adjustment of focus (by asking the question: Are we asking the right questions?).

These are resources which, in a less self-conscious and less developed way, we make use of all the time.

A single word is often used with a variety of slightly different meanings or without any very precise meaning at all. This is true of many of the terms we use in discussing art. 'Art' itself is an obvious example, but so are terms such as 'genius', 'beauty', 'quality', 'style' and 'expression'. In fact, few of the terms we use in such discussion have a plain and simple meaning. Conceptual analysis is the process by which we sort out the different meanings contained within a single term.

Chapter 2 provides a case study of this kind of analysis. The word 'art' is taken apart and a whole range of different meanings are distinguished; we can then sort through these and decide which we are really interested in and which are trivial. A word like 'art' is like a Swiss Army penknife. It is really a whole set of different implements welded together. When one person thinks of such a knife he may be interested in the corkscrew, while the person he is talking to is only interested in the nail file. But they think they are concerned with the same thing because they are both talking about a Swiss Army penknife. Conceptual analysis involves getting out all the blades and considering them separately, identifying each individually. So it is with a term like 'art'. One person uses it to signal quality, using 'art' as a term of *praise*. Another uses the term merely as a classification without any reference to quality. These two are bound to come to a misunderstanding, but it is a misunderstanding disguised by the use of a common term, 'art', a common term which disguises a difference of meaning.

Concepts are the building-blocks of thought. But thinking also involves putting concepts together and establishing connections and distinctions – in short, it involves argument: the process of reasoning. Argument should not be taken to imply two brutes going at each other hammer and tongs. Argument is the supporting of one idea on another; argument is the correct use of 'because'; argument is explanation; argument, at its best, is intellectual architecture. The second gift of philosophy is the evaluation of arguments. This is like the task of the structural engineer who has to come in to check that the concepts of the dreamy architect will actually stand up: the towers are lovely, but will they really stand firm upon such flimsy foundations?

The evaluation of arguments is an ancient science, one which was already well developed in the work of Plato and, particularly, Aristotle. It has personal application in considering the supportive or contradictory relations among one's own beliefs; it has wider application with respect to other people's thoughts. A standing characteristic of the human mind (although not a universal one) is that of being over-impressed by the arguments of others: they are liable to *sound* so authoritative and compelling. The evaluation of argument on its own merit is the counterweight to this. It allows us to gauge the intellectual authority of others not from their rhetorical forcefulness but upon the real strength (or weakness) of their chain of reasoning. This liberation constitutes one decisive step beyond intellectual adolescence.

The third gift of philosophy is harder to characterise. We, at times, puzzle over questions which seem to be of the first importance. Someone asks blankly: 'Am I happy?' or 'What is the meaning of life?' or 'How will I know when I have met the right partner?' The question may function as a subtle obstacle to further thought. Such questions cannot be answered (usually), while their apparent importance dazzles us. There are, however, related, simpler, more local questions which we could be getting on with were we not paralysed: 'Could I be content with Charlotte, whether or not she is ideal?', 'How serious am I about flying kites/gardening/collecting stamps – whether or not this constitutes the meaning of life?'

And so it often is in discussion of the arts. By asking the apparently crucial questions we paralyse ourselves; we put a stop to the discussion. To ask of some unlikely object, 'But is it art?' sounds as if the great question has been raised. But, so baldly posed, this question does not admit of a satisfying answer. There are more modest and more productive questions we could ask, such as: 'In what way is this object supposed to be valuable, and is it in fact valuable in that way?' or 'What different meanings does the word "art" have and which, if any, apply to this object?' There is no systematic approach to this slight shifting of focus from the paralysing question to the productive question. We can only cultivate a willingness to wonder whether the right questions are being asked.

These three virtues (analysis of concepts, evaluation of arguments and reflection on the focus of enquiry) are part-constitutive of the philosophical attitude in thinking. In drawing a portrait of painting *from a philosophical point of view* we shall be assessing the state of repair of the ideas (the tools) we use when we engage with paintings. And the aim of this undertaking is that we may better enjoy and appreciate paintings as works of art.

The black and white reproductions in this book aim to make intelligible the major points of discussion. But looking at any reproduction is different from contemplating a real painting. A real painting tends to look raw and crude in comparison with a glossy photograph and the small scale of reproduction makes it easier for the eye to take in the whole work at a single glance.

*

In writing this book I have been made aware of how much I owe to certain people and I should like to take this opportunity to express my gratitude to them, first to Anthony Grayling and the late Colin Haycraft who gave me the opportunity to write this book. My parents have always been supportive and encouraging, but their influence has been more specific than that: from my father I have acquired an intimacy with paintings, from my mother I have tried to learn how to speak about what I hold dear. I am particularly indebted for ideas and support to David Mayers and Alain de Botton. I am grateful also to Christopher Hamilton, Nigel Wentworth and Noga Arikha for encouragement at difficult moments. My most comprehensive intellectual debt is to Professor Malcolm Budd. One person has been taxed for support on quite another scale and to her this book is dedicated with love.

1

'Is It Any Good?':
Evaluating Art

1. Popping the question

Waiting for an Edgware train I survey the posters which solicit the free-floating mind of the underground passenger. One advertises a show of new painting: 'Explosive Work, Shocking and Provocative.' I gaze at the image of a shadowy figure, something like a black snowman, not easily distinguished from a primary school express-yourself-with-lots-of-lovely-paint experiment. The poster tells me that the work is 'subversive and provocative'. Litter on the heath, miscarriages of justice and people who don't turn up for dinner are subversive and provocative, but one has no inclination to rate these things highly. The disturbing question forms itself: 'Is this new work any good?' or, to put it another way, 'Are these good paintings?'[1]

Whether something is good or not is one of the most natural questions we can raise; our capacity to pursue an answer sincerely and patiently is a triumph of civilisation. A simple 'yes' or 'no' response, in the present case, would not be very interesting. We might wonder why this is. After all, with many questions which have the form: 'is this ...' or 'is it ...' we are quite happy with a 'yes' or 'no' answer: 'Is this the bus to Gospel Oak?' or 'Is this seat free?' Why is it uninteresting to answer our question in this way?

Philosophers who love distinctions have drawn attention to a difference between asking 'Is this tennis racket any good?' and asking 'Is this painting any good?' In the first case we have, more or less, a clear notion of what is involved in a racket being a *good* tennis racket: it must be balanced, light, strong and have a comfortable tension in the strings. We do not have the same sort of tick-list of features which make a picture good: some excellent pictures are realistic, some are not, some fine paintings involve a luscious texture of paint, some do not. Simply being told that a picture is good, is not very helpful. So, what sort of answer am I looking for when I ask of a painting 'Is it any good?'[2]

I am asking for an *explanation* of how and why I should find this thing valuable. I want an account of why someone might care for this picture, hang it on the wall, pay money for it, think it important; and I want to consider whether I too might care for it and in what way. What does the object promise me, what does it offer? I am looking for an answer which will explain how I might appreciate the work. Often the explanation offered is unsatisfactory; that is what I felt about the underground poster. For merely being 'provocative' does not explain why I should care about the painting. There are many provocative things I think it is important to hate and object to. In the absence of explanation, my scepticism flourishes.

The demand for explanation is just as strong when it comes to the great works of tradition. Just what is so good about Monet or Frans Hals? This is not a dismissive question: it is a genuine plea for explanation. If these painters really have produced works of great value – and they have – then we should be able to explain to ourselves what it is about their work that is so valuable. Answering this question will not be some dry academic exercise to be performed once by some scholar so that when it is done we can all sit back comfortably in the belief that the value of these works has been explained. The point is that if we are to *make that value our own*, if we are to appreciate the work, we must in some sense be able to explain *to ourselves* what is valuable about the work.

The same demand for an explanatory answer to the question 'Is it any good?' is raised both by the unfamiliar work of the present day and by the traditionally accepted work of the past. In both cases we want to understand what of value these works offer the beholder.

Asking whether something is any good risks the answer that, in the end, it isn't much good and consequently hurting someone's feelings. This is not a pleasant risk to run. It is not polite to ask if a picture is any good; it is not polite even to wonder quietly to oneself.

2. The Aquinas Complex

It is not enough for us merely to love or hate something: a person, a picture, a place; it is one of the splendours and miseries of human nature that we seek to justify our likes and dislikes, our passions and attachments. I hate Charlotte's friends *because* they are all snobs; I love Corot's picture of Avignon, *Avignon from the West* (plate 1), because it looks just like the real thing; this country is falling apart *because* a bunch of crooks are in power. The quality of reason-giving may vary, but addiction to it is standard, if not universal.

It is splendid that we go in for reason-giving. It is miserable that the reasons we offer ourselves and others are often so poor: so often they are obviously exercises in self-deception, or they involve clutching at the first cliché which presents itself. We are not good at giving *good* reasons for our evaluations.

We try to explain our passions primarily in what could be called 'objective' terms. Thinking that an act of wanton cruelty is morally outrageous, you rebel against the thought that there is nothing wrong with the act and that something is wrong with you: you are over-sensitive. Our moral evaluations present themselves as judgments about how things are in the world, *not* as expressions of private and merely personal responses.

It is not only sombre judgments that present themselves in this light. Suppose (philosophy thrives on imagination) I am not enjoying eating the mange-tout peas, this is because (I tell myself) they have been over-cooked. There is something about them, about the green things on my plate, which explains my negative response. It is so much less satisfying to think that there is nothing wrong with them – that, on the contrary, there is something wrong with me: I am fussy.

The rights and wrongs of this domestic crisis are not important. What is important is that it shows we have an instinctive response to the Aquinas Complex: 'Do we like X (Charlotte, the picture, the government) because it *is* good, or do we just *think* X is good because we like it?' Human instinct as manifest in the mange-tout episode is firmly in favour of the first view: I dislike the peas *because* there is something awry with them (they have been over-cooked). We are by instinct resistant to the second option: I only *think* there is a problem with them *because of something about me*.

The explanation we want is one couched in terms of the good (or bad) qualities of the object. When I look at *Avignon from the West*, I am impressed by the perfect harmony between the undulating horizontals of the various recessions of depth; the more steeply rising and falling crests of the foreground, and the serene gentleness of the far hills, are perfectly balanced by the short verticals of the Papal palace; there are lovely transitions in focus: the nearer ground is roughly depicted, almost sketched in, which lends a contrastive clarity to the mediaeval buildings; the evocation of sunlight and time of day, and the depiction of distance over which the eye travels, are simply and completely achieved. This explanation of my finding the picture valuable consists solely of the catalogue of good qualities of the object: features which are there for anyone to discover.

3. Appreciation

'... Because you were kept guessing who the real murderer was, of course you're supposed to think it was Macbeth, then Lady Macbeth perhaps.' The speaker preens herself on 'spotting' that it was the Doctor of Physic, a minor figure who appears only in Act V. This is one way of enjoying the play, but it hardly counts as appreciating Shakespeare. Why not? Answering this question requires a definition of 'appreciation'.

The notion of appreciation is one of the most poignant and inspiring that we have. When Charlotte says 'You don't appreciate me' the implication is that she has real qualities the value of which is being ignored. Thus, to appreciate is to grasp the valuable qualities of something or someone. The note of tragedy is sounded when we recognise that we did not appreciate some good when we had the chance, and it is only later, once it is lost, that the failure to appreciate becomes agonisingly apparent. Often it takes loss to make us see what we should have appreciated. This can act, too, as an inspiration: it awakens in us the desire, the longing, to appreciate now what goods we have, and thus to avoid the repetition of the tragedy.

People use the term 'appreciation' in different ways. Sometimes it is used as a mere synonym for 'like' or 'enjoy'. In providing a definition of 'appreciation' I shall not try to do justice to every single legitimate use of the word. Rather, I shall try to capture just one central idea which we can get at with this word. It is this idea and not the word itself which is important.

T.S. Eliot defines 'appreciation' as 'liking something for the right reasons'. The woman who likes *Macbeth* 'because you have to work out who killed Duncan' certainly likes the play but she does not like it for the right reasons. The reason she cites does not apply to the play at all.

It is a favourite device of novelists to set their characters at cross purposes. Lord S feels pity for B because he *thinks* she has been maltreated by her husband. In fact her husband has behaved admirably. Lord S's reason for feeling sorry for B is *mistaken*: he has a mistaken reason for feeling pity. That reason for pity would only have been a right reason if B's husband had *in fact* behaved badly. So it is with appreciation: the reasons in question must be true of the thing appreciated. Appreciation is always cast in terms of qualities which the object really does have. This is central to distinguishing it from mere liking. After all, I can like someone because I am under an illusion about their good qualities. But this would not be a case of appreciation, for I can only appreciate a person for qualities he actually does have.

A proffered reason (for *p*'s having artistic merit) must satisfy two conditions. First, it must actually apply to the work in question. But this is not all. A proffered reason might correctly apply to the work but not be of the appropriate kind to establish *p* as artistically valuable. If I say '*p* was bought by the Duke of Brabant, therefore *p* has high artistic merit', it is obvious that the cited fact is inappropriate for establishing artistic merit.

The term appreciation derives from the late Latin *appretiare*, which means 'to set a price on something'. This is equally applicable whether it is a high or a low price which is set. The implication is of judging the value of something, whether that value be low or high. It is a quirk of English that 'appreciation' is generally used only with a positive sense of putting a high value on something, although outside the arts it is used, as in 'I appreciate the gravity of the situation', to express a grasp of how bad something is. It is helpful even in discussion of the arts to retain this more flexible use. Seeing what is so bad about one painting is intimately connected with seeing what is so good about another. Appreciating the fineness of one thing requires that we appreciate when another is not fine. We could usefully speak of appreciating the artistic failure of a work: meaning that we grasp its low value as a work of art.

The reference to enjoyment in Eliot's formulation has disappeared; we are now talking about reasons for valuing rather than reasons for liking or enjoying. This is an advance. Sometimes we may think that a painting is of the highest artistic value and yet not enjoy looking at it. Sometimes this happens because the subject matter of the work is so grave. In *The Idiot*, Dostoevsky has one of his characters reflect on Holbein's famous picture *The Dead Man*, which has often been understood as a picture of the dead Christ.

> And if the master himself, on the eve of his execution, could have seen this image, would he have mounted the cross as he did, and died as he did? This question too is bound to come to mind as you look at the picture.[3]

It is clear that this picture has made a tremendous impact, and let us suppose for the sake of argument that this is a valid interpretation of the work. The speaker sets a high value on the work, but it would be misleading to say that he enjoys looking at it. All the same, we often do value paintings in part because of the enjoyment of looking at them. Emphasis on valuing a work does not exclude pleasure as *one way* of valuing a work of art.

There is a world of a difference between actually finding something valuable oneself and merely asserting that something is valuable (but not on the basis of one's own experience). If it is true that an object is valuable, then I can know that it is valuable, having been informed of this by others, without finding it valuable myself. Thus valuing something is not the same as just believing it to be valuable. This point might sound slight, but it is actually very important. When I find something valuable the explanation of why it is valuable is open to me and draws upon my own experience. Otherwise I am stranded at the end of someone else's judgment. The tourists in the Louvre, joining the crowd in front of the *Mona Lisa*, quite rightly believe that they are standing before a work of the highest artistic value. But what is that to them if they cannot recover in their own experience why it is valuable, if they cannot find it valuable themselves? To speak metaphorically, it is the difference between being inside, with the value, and just seeing it from the outside. One of the greatest aims of life is to experience value from the inside, as one's own.

The notion of appreciation which we are working with here is expressed as 'valuing something for the right reasons'. Something has been said about valuing, but attention must now be paid to the phrase 'for the right reasons'. Use of such a phrase is liable to make questions flare up: 'But what are the right reasons, and how do we know that they are right? Who decides what the right reasons are?' Often the questions are raised with the expectation that no answer can be forthcoming and that at their trumpeting the walls of pretention will at once collapse.

This small river of questions is an intellectual Rubicon and it is no simple matter to make one's way securely across. The fording point comes when we realise that the reference to a particular person is out of place. Framing the question in terms of 'who' is misleading. For the *justification* of the judgment of quality is independent of *who* happens to provide it. When I was trying to explain why *Avignon from the West* is such a good picture, it did not count for much that it was *I* who said those things, all that mattered was *what* I said. The question 'Who decides?' trades on the assumption that all that matters is *who* asserts a value judgment, as if we could never consider whether the reasons offered are convincing apart from the identity of the person who happens to express them.

The question 'Who decides?' is not usually asked in the spirit of open-minded empirical enquiry. It is an aggressive question which supposes the following. First, that there is a person, or set of persons, who *decide* what is or is not of high artistic merit. Secondly, that their decisions mean that artistic excellence does not really belong to the work. Thirdly, that the decision is supported by an agenda which, in itself, has nothing to do with art. The 'decision' is always subservient to that agenda, and asking 'Who decides?' is a way of unmasking the presence of this agenda.

At its heart, this is an alienated way of thinking. What would make someone suppose that there is no possibility of spontaneously and freely finding something excellent? Perhaps never having had this experience for themselves. The alienation resides in the underlying thought that high esteem could not be given unless there were a pay-off for the giver (in this scenario, the advance of a hidden agenda). But this suggests that the critical voice has never itself experienced a freely given high regard, without the suspicion that there must be something in it for the giver, some dubious advantage to be gained.

This private difficulty might have led to a yearning to develop the capacity for free and spontaneous admiration. Instead, with the aggressive question 'Who decides?' the personal dissatisfaction is shrugged off and projected onto everyone else. 'I can only like a work if there is some ideological advantage in it for me, therefore the reason why anyone gives high esteem to a work is because it suits their hidden agenda, therefore the works which are publicly esteemed are so only because someone decides that they should be, and decides on an ideological basis.'

There is always a distinction to be drawn between the artistic excellence of a work and the social recognition of it. The history of what gets recognised as excellent is interesting, and of course this history depends upon the fluctuations of political power and propaganda.

But aside from this troubled history there is the fixed heaven of what is artistically excellent; what is there to be recognised as such – whether or not it is so recognised. The works of Vermeer were artistically excellent all through the nineteenth century when they were not recognised as great works. Sentimental or crudely bombastic works may, for a while, achieve great status, but they are never artistically excellent, no matter what acclaim they are greeted with. Acclaim can be misplaced, recognition can miss the best objects. If one accepts these two fundamental possibilities, then one accepts that artistic excellence is not grounded in a set of 'decisions' about what is artistically excellent.

4. Valuable as what exactly?

There is a poster on the underground advertising special delivery for precious goods. It shows a lopsided blue mug decorated with yellow stars and a note 'To Grandma, love Ben'. The mug is valued as a token of affection or for the painstaking labour of little Ben which produced it. By contrast it is not valued *as* a mug, for it will not sit stably on the table and something went wrong with the clay that forms the base so the tea will leak out. When we appreciate or value something we always appreciate it *as a such-and-such*. Some phrase such as 'as a token of love', 'as a drinking vessel', is always implied, even though context may make it unnecessary to state this sortal phrase. When Grandma says she really appreciated Ben's gift we know that she means 'as a token of affection'.

Right reasons for valuing the object have to reflect what it is being valued *as*. Thus, if Grandma values Ben's mug *as* a token of affection, it just does not matter that the mug is lopsided. On the other hand, should she value the mug *as* a drinking vessel, it would not matter that little Ben devoted hours to making it. Nothing can be valuable as a drinking vessel *just because* someone devoted all afternoon to making it.

The question in play is 'What makes a reason a correct reason for valuing a painting?' The answer, it is now apparent, will depend upon what the painting is being valued *as*. If we are valuing it as an investment, then the name of the artist will matter a good deal, and whether that artist's reputation is growing or declining will matter even more.

A collector may value a particular picture because it was owned by Madame de Pompadour. In this case, the right reason for valuing the picture is just that it was owned by that woman.

When we talk about valuing a painting, however, it is generally implied that we are concerned with its value 'as a work of art'. And it is with this that we shall be exclusively concerned here. Yet it is not clear what the consequences of this phrase are. The notion of 'art' is a fairly vague one, so it is not clear exactly what is meant when we speak of valuing something *as a work of art*. The next chapter will continue with the task of elucidating a notion of 'valuing something as a work of art'. Only once that sortal phrase is elucidated can we go on to say with precision what is relevant to valuing a picture *as a work of art*. But before we turn to that delicate operation, there are two further features of the notion of appreciation to which attention must be drawn.

5. Appreciation and life

A submerged, but highly significant, point is that the appreciation of X (a painting, a person, a gift) filters out into the rest of life. One way in which it does this is through a sort of ranking of appreciations. Imagine you give someone (dear, darling Y) a carefully chosen, expensive and beautifully wrapped present which, you happily feel, perfectly expresses your depth of feeling towards her. Receiving the present Y is delighted, attentive to the wrapping, subtly aware of the expense and sensitive to the intention. Everything is perfect, Y appreciates your gift. But then your rival brings forward a crumpled packet containing a novelty, and Y, to your horror, is just as delighted. If she ranks these together, then she cannot have appreciated your gift. This subtle complaint was perfectly expressed by Browning:

> She had a heart – how shall I say? – too soon made glad,
> Too easily impressed; she liked whate'er
> She looked on and her looks went everywhere.
> Sir, 't was all one![4]

Appreciation spins out into behaviour and life. If I am really to appreciate the value of something, I must be prepared to value it above other things. I must say that it is more important than something else, and I must act in line with this. This is an aspect of really finding something valuable, and not just asserting that one does so. It is not always easy to draw this distinction in practice, because we are so good sometimes at deceiving ourselves. We so much want to put a high value on something that we convince ourselves that we do. But the proof comes in action, and unless by our actions we show that we do put a high value on this thing, then we are to some extent deluding ourselves.

The aim of reflecting on appreciation is not only intellectual: it is not only to understand this interesting and difficult concept that the task is undertaken. There is also a practical aim: to make genuine appreciation possible, to end up experiencing value from the inside, making it one's own.

All the talk so far about reason-giving and the justification of judgments about artistic quality might seem far from the actual experience of art; that experience is best described as just letting the picture make its impact, some will say. But if we think about the matter, the two (justification and impact) are not really opposed. For the reason-giving is just a way of *reporting* what it was about the picture which made an impact. When I *look* at the Corot I enjoy the appearance of the juxtaposition of horizontal and vertical accents, the sense of distance and recession of plane. I don't need to be talking to myself about these when I look. If, later, I want to *justify* the judgment that the Corot is a fine painting, I can indicate what it was about the picture that made such an impact. Those features are cited as reasons in support of a judgment of quality.

Criticism, in one of its better guises, is a way of trying to be self-conscious about evaluations: a picture makes an impact; well, what sort of impact, and what is it about the picture which is so striking? While clearly not mandatory, there is nevertheless no ground for supposing that being self-conscious about looking at a picture makes one less sensitive to it. Confusion arises because people sometimes get nervous in front of a picture and that sort of self-consciousness – 'What am I supposed to like about this, I don't understand, what should I be looking at, am I missing the point?' – does prevent the person from appreciating the painting: but that is not the sort of self-consciousness with which I am concerned.

The best sort of criticism does not seek to set out *rules*

for appreciation, or about what makes a painting artistically excellent; rather, it aims to bring to our attention what is fine about a particular work and to develop our capacity to appreciate: not judging for us, but enabling us to judge for ourselves. But judging seriously for ourselves is not something we should expect to be able to do 'without thought or lecture'. In later chapters we shall discuss in more detail how it is that judgments of artistic excellence are justified and how an appreciative eye develops.

Notes

1. When we ask of a picture 'Is it any good?' it is *implied* that we are asking whether the painting is any good *as a work of art*. It is far from obvious what the precise significance of this implied phrase, 'as a work of art', is. It will be discussed at length in Chapter 2. For the time being I just note its presence in the wings.

2. Language provides for at least two rather different ways in which we can use the word 'good'. We can simply say that something is good, or we can say that it is good as a such and such, under a *sortal phrase* such as 'as a cricketer'. We can say that Simon is good, or we can say that he is good as a cricketer, that is, good at playing cricket. It may be, however, that this linguistic difference is only a superficial quirk, and that when we say, simply, 'Simon is good' we imply 'as a man' or 'as a person' or some such sortal phrase.

3. Feodor Dostoevsky, *The Idiot*, translated by Alan Myers, Oxford University Press, 1992, p. 431.

4. Robert Browning, 'My Last Duchess' in *The New Book of English Verse*, ed. Helen Gardner, Oxford University Press, 1972.

2

The Idea of Art

1. Asking the right question

It is a pleasant summer evening for an Art School Finals show. Along the appealing and unfamiliar succession of rooms a few items are attracting special notice. Some vacuum cleaners have been heaped or placed in a perspex container about the size of a bath but standing on one end. This is catalogued under the title 'Untitled Multiple Perspexive'. The question 'But is it art?' is forming itself in some irreverent heads. If you knew about these things you would know that K – its creator – is set to be one of the most recognised new artists. It is not hard to understand this object. Not so long ago someone exhibited some dirty carpets rolled up in filing cabinets – what a stink that caused. But now art is mawkishly cleaning itself up: 'You didn't like our dirty carpets, well, see, we can clean them up for you.' And the sophisticate knows that this is yet another example of art playing cat and mouse with bourgeois expectations.

'And the perspex?'

'Simple. Obviously a pun on Brunelleschi's *perspective* by which he tried to render (and control) the external world. K's *perspexive* renders the inner world. With Brunelleschi you have to adopt the monocular vision of the male point of view, but with K's perspex all points of view are equal.'

But still comes the question 'Is it art?' What does the questioner want?

The question 'But is it art?' has become a cliché. It is a pat response to the more bizarre and arcane objects encountered in galleries. What makes it a cliché is that no one answers it, and no one is expected to answer it. It has degenerated into a polite exit line: 'I do like art you know, I'm no philistine, and *if* this is art, I'll take it seriously and do my best to like it, only I'm not altogether sure it is art.' Face is saved.

On the surface, the question 'But is it art?' is of the same *kind* as the question 'But is it a plant?' The sea-anemone was so called because ancient biologists thought that it looked like the familiar anemone plant. At some point someone asked the crucial question, 'But is it a plant?' Upon investigation it was discovered that the sea-anemone is in fact an animal, and what were thought to be stamens turned out to be tentacles.

The question 'But is it a plant?' is a question about the *application* of a general term in a specific case. The difficulty lies with the fact that it is not easy to tell whether this thing (this little object in the water) really does possess the features which plants have and so belong to the plant kingdom.

When we ask of the piled-up vacuum cleaners 'But is it art?' the situation is superficially similar, but actually radically different. For in this case we do not have a clear and simple account of *what we mean by 'art'*. Supposing someone said to the biologist: 'OK, you are wondering whether this thing in the sea is a *plant*. Well, what do you mean by "plant"?' The biologist could have given a pretty good answer: something which has chlorophyll, and a certain sort of cellular structure, and so on. It doesn't matter that this definition is too crude for some very tricky cases. It suffices to explain broadly what is at stake in the question 'Is this a plant?'

By contrast, when the question comes back 'But what do you mean by "art"?' the chances of a straightforward answer are pretty slim. Mostly people ask 'But is it art?' precisely *because* they are not sure what they mean by 'art'. Before getting to grips with what is at stake in the question 'But is it art?' we must get to grips with the logically prior question 'But what do you mean by "art"?'

2. Words versus ideas

The history of the term 'art' has received a great deal of academic study. It is striking how varied the uses of the term have been. For example:

(i) 'Art' has been used almost as a synonym for 'craft', as in the art of shoemaking – and so could be used to highlight the skill involved in making a fine painting.

(ii) At a later stage, 'art' came to be contrasted with 'craft': art was the realm of inspiration and genius. Although this opposition has itself a long history it is particularly linked with Romanticism.

(iii) For centuries it was orthodox to hold that art was intimately linked with representation, the art of painting was the art of rendering the visible world by means of pigment on a flat surface. There was a period when art was identified with expression, and more recently the connections with both representation and expression have been questioned.

(iv) For almost all of its history the term 'art' has been one of praise. Comparatively recently, however, this has changed. When Duchamp sought to have his 'Urinal' accepted as a work of art, he did not mean that the object should be praised for its niceties of design (which had never been denied). Rather he wanted it to bludgeon its way into a select circle. Just as the term 'aristocrat' is not a term of praise but of privilege, so 'art' has been used to present objects as having a special status, but not because they are good or fine objects, any more than someone can qualify for the status of aristocrat on the basis of his or her fine or good qualities.

What are we to make of all these conflicting uses: what point could there possibly be to a term which can be used to mean all these different things?

One option is to try to discern some pattern in these shifts. 'After all,' some will say, 'the word did not have all these meanings at the same time. Its significance has been changing over time, as art itself has changed.' The rapid changes in aims and concerns exhibited by people called 'artists' in this century have encouraged such views. Everyone would like to be able to second-guess where art will go next, and riches await the person who is first to discern, or even better to initiate a new twist in the story.

However, this whole view, popular as it is, rests upon a misconception. It is one thing to point out that a word has undergone a shift in meaning. It is quite another to claim that a concept has developed. This is obvious when we look at a banal example. The word 'competitor' in the sixteenth century had the connotation of 'one associated with another in seeking a common object; an associate, a partner'. Since then this usage has become obsolete and 'competitor' now connotes rivalry. Some may claim to see a change 'in the very notion of competition'. They might claim to see in this linguistic shift a lamentable sign of the increasing rivalry of the modern world. Such a conclusion would be entirely out of order.

It is still perfectly possible to express the *idea* or *concept* of a partner in a joint endeavour, it is only that a different *form of words* is now used to do so. The fallacy lies in identifying a concept or idea with a single word and then supposing that if the word (the string of letters) changes its significance the concept or idea has changed. This is obviously unjustified, for a concept or idea can be expressed in a variety of ways and so cannot be identified with any single string of letters. Thus we are perfectly well able to express the *idea* of a representation of the world rendered in pigment on a flat surface, only we no longer use the word 'art' to designate that activity.

The fact is that there is no single idea expressed exclusively by the term 'art'. The word is no more powerful than the ideas we use it to express. There are just different conceptions which are found to be more or less useful, and they all compete for attention. The set of available ideas remains relatively stable, it is only *which* idea the string of letters 'a-r-t' picks out that has changed. This is also true of the string of letters 'c-o-m-p-e-t-i-t-o-r'.

If we are to makes sense of what is at stake when it is asked of K's *Perspexive* 'But is it art?' we need to look at the underlying ideas: what, if any, important underlying ideas does the word 'art' stand for in this question?

3. Putting the Artworld first

When faced with all the different concepts which have been linked with the word 'art', and giving up on the hope of finding a pattern of development among them, another option is to try to find a 'common factor' among all of those uses. But what could they possibly have in common?

It has been suggested that the common factor is just this: an object is designated by certain people as a candidate for appreciation in some way. The people in question are those belonging to the 'Artworld'. And who are they? Today they are just whoever take themselves to be concerned about 'art': the minimum requirement for entry to this world is simply that one uses the key term 'art'. The objects which are so designated by these people are, by definition, works of art.

This represents an extreme liberal position: anything can be a work of art. The underlying thought is quite simple: what we are trying to do, its supporter will say, is just explain how the word 'art' is used and always has been used – namely that some people use it of certain things. There is a certain anthropological toughness about this answer: 'We're just studying what people do, we're not concerned about whether it makes any sense, that's not for us to judge, and this is what people do.'

Going back to the *Untitled Multiple Perspexive*, it is now very easy to answer the question 'But is it art?' This object is called 'art' by some members of the Artworld; some people who use the word 'art' use it of this thing. However, the ease with which the answer is given undermines the point of giving it. It does nothing to respond to the spirit of the original question simply to point out that some people are prepared to attach a particular label to the object. The reply must come back: 'So what?' On the current view the word 'art' is just like a green star. At primary school we used to be given stars – a gold star or a silver star gummed onto the page when our work was correct or neat or showed signs of effort. One day people started to get green stars, but no one could say with certainty what they were *for*. There was no quality or achievement of which the green star was a recognition: it merely showed that the teacher had put a green star on the page. However, this does not stop the green star having, at first, a mysterious glamour. Being a member of the Artworld is like having a packet of green stars and a licence to apply them at will.

This reveals a fault-line in the rhetoric of contemporary art. One critic, writing in *The People's Artworld*, claimed that K's work 'challenged the boundaries of art'. But what does this 'challenge' amount to? It adds up to no more than the remark that K put a green star on something no one had thought of putting a green star on before: a mediocre accomplishment. It is impossible to have both an 'all things to all men' attitude towards the word 'art', following some sort of misplaced democratic urge – 'art belongs to the people, it is whatever we want it to be' – and a conviction that it matters whether something is 'art' or not. In fact it is *not* impossible, only incoherent.

The rest of this chapter is concerned with setting out what I take to be two central concerns which the word 'art' can be used to indicate, which are fundamental to what we are getting at when we talk of 'appreciating something *as a work of art*': concerns with intrinsic value and with irreplaceability. In the next chapter, I shall discuss a third central concern: artistry. The word 'art' has now become too debased to represent these concerns without confusion. But this does nothing at all to detract from their centrality. It is these concerns which underlie the question 'But is it art?' The heart of that question is 'Does this object have intrinsic value, is it irreplaceable and has artistry been exercised in the creation of such value?' In another sense, 'But is it art?' it is not really a question at all: it is an expression of scepticism – it expresses the doubt that K, in making *Untitled Multiple Perspexive*, has, with an exercise of artistry, made something which is of intrinsic and irreplaceable value.

4. Intrinsic value

Prague can still be cold at the end of April, and rain leaves even the Charles Bridge quiet. Having crossed from the New Town I turn left into a side street, looking for a spire first seen from across the Vlatva. Under my umbrella a private space forms. The lane opens into a small square. On the farther side a window is open, above head height, intimating a dim and tranquil inner space, like the Academy Life Room when the students have gone. Someone is practising the violin and I imagine the musician's feeling for the room, feelings for its old windows, for the bookcases in the dim natural light, for textures and for the wear of wood giving each thing an individual curve: a feeling for the intrinsic value of things, the value which each thing has as irreplaceable; an eye filled with love settles on the individuality of each object, the little details of difference which distinguish it from others of its kind. A chair, here, is not just a chair, but *the* chair with its own known particular detail: a piece of braid, a split opening, the idiosyncrasy of the joints, even the way dust has settled into the simple carvings, these would be missed if the chair were replaced by 'something else to sit on'. Intrinsic value is contrasted with functional value. Another chair may be just as comfortable to sit on (or even more so), and yet, beyond its capacity to perform this function (of providing a place to sit comfortably), this chair has a value for us. That value is bound up with the way the chair looks; the pleasure of setting eyes upon it is independent of the satisfaction of sitting on it.

There are ways in which almost any object can be *invested* with intrinsic value. A child's security blanket is like this: it is irreplaceable because the child has invested it with special importance. It is not as if the child has noticed, with infant discernment, a special quality of the blanket. The child is doing something very important with this object, but the same could have been done with something else. It is only as the investment is made that the object acquires intrinsic value. Before that investment the object simply did not have this value.

By contrast there are ways in which we *notice* intrinsic value: when we come to know and care for a person or a stretch of countryside or a quarter of a city. It is this last, the *noticing* of the intrinsic value of something, which is the most important notion we can have in connection with works of art. For these are objects which, for the most part, have been created either entirely or largely for the sake of their intrinsic value: for the satisfaction which can be derived merely by contemplating them, and not from the further tasks they might perform.

Intrinsic value is essentially experiential – it has to be or the object would be, in principle, only a means to something else, and therefore replaceable. Only the experience of *that* object cannot be replaced. What has sometimes been called 'aesthetic experience' would count as an *instance* of experiencing intrinsic value. The notion of aesthetic experience was developed in the eighteenth century to try to capture ways in which the experience of some objects (certain pictures, sculpture, music, poetry, sunsets, trees and so on) differs from other sorts of experience, for example, moral sentiment or sensuous pleasure. This project of drawing fine discriminations among kinds of experience is quite compatible with the broad claim, made here, that it is characteristic of paintings, drawings and so on (in short, the arts) that they serve the experience of intrinsic value.

Intrinsic value is not unique to objects which are called 'works of art'. Most objects can be discovered to have some intrinsic value, but usually only to a small degree. For example, a nicely designed glass cannot be replaced without loss except by another glass of the same type. Another kind of glass might be preferred, but it will not have just those qualities. Some qualities, therefore, will be lost to us when we replace the glass with one of another kind, although further and new qualities will be gained. I do care about the design, and hence about the intrinsic value, of the glass on the desk in front of me: it is not only a receptacle for water or wine. If we take intrinsic value to be the central value of works of art we are in the happy position of recognising a continuity between the value of works of art and the value of humbler everyday objects.

To put things more technically: often we value one thing *because* we value something else. Someone asks, why do you value having a certain kind of chair? Because it is comfortable to sit on for long periods, something my work requires me to do. In this case my valuing the chair requires reference to something else that I value: physical comfort. In this way the chair is regarded functionally, as a means to an end. By contrast, when we regard something as intrinsically valuable, we are not concerned about anything else which we value. If I just like looking at the chair because it has a pleasing shape then there is no further thing I am valuing and in virtue of which I regard the chair as valuable. Once we start to think about it, there are many things which we value *both* functionally and intrinsically. I go swimming both because it is healthy (a means to being healthy) and because I enjoy it for its own sake: I like the feel of the water and the sensation of being supported by it.

Intrinsic value is a kind of value, not a degree. That is, something may have a very low intrinsic value and still be valued that way.

5. Irreplaceability

When a picture is valued as a work of art, it is valued as irreplaceable. If it is not valued as irreplaceable then we are not concerned about it as a work of art. When a picture is valued as irreplaceable, it is regarded in such a way that no other thing could be valuable in just that way. This is, in fact, typical of the way we regard the paintings in the National Gallery. Any visible change to the surface of a work by, say, Vermeer or Velásquez would alter the artistic value of the work. These are pictures in which every visible element counts – change one and the effect ripples out. Suppose the pink of the ribbons in Velásquez's *Rokeby Venus* (plate 13) were changed, then the harmony between the ribbon and the curtains would be altered, and the link between the ribbon and the bloom of the girl's cheek would be changed. The very precise artistic merits of the work depend upon its having just the visible properties it does have. This means that if one of the visible properties is changed, then the precise artistic merits of the work will change. Thus, when the picture is valued for those artistic merits, it is valued as irreplaceable.[1]

The point about irreplaceability – and its centrality in understanding what it is to appreciate a picture as a work of art – can be made in a slightly different way. When I appreciate a painting as a work of art, it is necessary that I appreciate it, in part, for its aesthetic properties. In making this claim I am using the term 'aesthetic property' in a specialised way which requires explanation. The notion of an aesthetic property can be given a precise technical meaning, and a little care is required in spelling out that meaning. We can close in on this notion by first considering the *genus*, or larger class, of properties to which it belongs. When I say that a picture is predominantly yellow, I am attributing a perceptual property to it. The standard way in which such a property is attributed is on the basis of perceptual experience. What it is for a picture to be predominantly yellow is for it to *look* predominantly yellow. Nothing is simpler to imagine than the case of someone saying 'That picture is predominantly yellow' on the basis of his visual experience.

Aesthetic properties are special in that they are dependent not just upon perceptual experience, but specifically upon a feeling of pleasure or pain connected with that experience, if they are to be correctly attributed. What is it to find a picture graceful? Well, the gracefulness of the lines in *The Rokeby Venus* is something one can see. But anyone who calls those lines graceful implies that they experience pleasure when looking at them. If someone who contemplated those lines and was utterly bored by them were to turn round and say 'Aren't they graceful!' he would be misusing the term (supposing he was not being ironic). It is this dependence upon pleasurable or unpleasurable experience, for their proper predication, which marks out aesthetic properties. A property is aesthetic if it is properly predicated on the basis of a pleasurable or unpleasurable perception.[2]

This two-fold condition, perception and pleasure or pain, is present in the etymology of the word 'aesthetic' itself. In Greek, the word *aisthesis* was used to refer to perception: hearing and seeing were central cases of *aisthesis*. In eighteenth-century Germany, the term was used to refer especially to the experience of pleasure and pain. This was the way Baumgarten, who is credited with the foundation of the modern subject of Aesthetics, used the term. The technical use that I have just described thus combines these two concerns: perception and pleasure or pain.

Paintings, it has already been claimed, are valued as works of art only when we are concerned with their aesthetic features.[3] We can now see that the aesthetic properties of a work depend upon its precise visual appearance. If you alter a graceful line it cannot remain graceful in just the way it was. If it is still graceful, it is with a slightly different grace. When a painting is valued for its aesthetic properties it is valued as irreplaceable.[4] To value a painting as a work of art we must be concerned with its aesthetic properties. Therefore when a painting is valued as a work of art it is necessarily valued as irreplaceable.

Not everything which is regarded as having intrinsic value is regarded as irreplaceable. I regard the cup and saucer before me as having a certain intrinsic value: I chose them not only because they serve their function as a drinking vessel but also because I think they look nice – something which I value for its own sake. But were I to knock over the cup in front of me it would not occasion much regret. For I fully believe that another cup and saucer in the cupboard will preserve exactly the same intrinsic value.

When we are appreciating a painting as a work of art it is usually as irreplaceable: nothing else could have just that intrinsic value.

6. Functional art: a contradiction?

In the Louvre, the *Winged Victory of Samothrace* with a graceful swing of her hips still alights blithe and elysian at the head of the monumental steps which lead to the Grand Galerie and the Galerie d'Apollon. Every day thousands pass; do any stop to ask 'But is it art?' Perhaps they should, for its creator did not have access to the term 'art'. And it might be thought that one can only make a work of art if one can wield the term 'art'. However that problem is resolved (or accommodated), there is no need for the specific term 'art' in order to produce or enjoy an object for its intrinsic and irreplaceable value and for the artistry which went into its making. The *Victory* was made to be looked at and enjoyed for how it looks, for the perceptual experience it furnishes – that is, for its intrinsic and irreplaceable merits. This is true even though the statue had *functions* too. It was made to celebrate a victory: perhaps it was commissioned by opportunist leaders who wanted to make the most of their advantage; perhaps it was made to propagate an ideology of war and triumph. All of these provide *functions* which, as things turn out, that statue is able to satisfy. But other statues could have fulfilled those functions. This particular statue, the remains of which are admired today in Paris, was *replaceable without loss* as far as those functions are concerned. It was only with regard to its appearance that it was not replaceable. Intrinsic value does not belong to an object in opposition to its functional value: it is not the case that the more an object fulfils functions the *less* its intrinsic value. Equally it is not the case (as the most naive of Functionalist architects claimed) that intrinsic value increases with the fulfilment of functional aims. Both are wrong for the same reason: intrinsic value is *independent* of function.

The notion of intrinsic value sets forth a central way in which objects can be valuable. It does not cover everything which has been called 'art'. If, as has just been admitted, it is not true that all things *called* 'works of art' *are* made wholly or primarily for the sake of intrinsic value, what can be the authority of the claim that serving intrinsic value is characteristic of painting, drawing, sculpture and the other arts? The focus of interest, however, is *not* the class of objects which are *called* 'art'.

The distinction between intrinsic and functional value is more important than that between what is called 'art' and what is not called 'art'. What has really mattered to us about the paintings of the past is the way they achieved intrinsic value: this is still the way in which pictures come to be valuable now. If a term like 'art' loses contact with the principal ways in which objects can matter to us, then it matters less and less whether an object has that thin label attached to it, for no label can conjure value into existence and the want of a label cannot remove from an object the intrinsic value it possesses.

7. Conclusion

In this chapter we have tried to understand what it is to value a painting 'as a work of art'. Our interest in this was prompted by the formulation of appreciation as valuing something for the right reasons. But it then became apparent that the notion of 'right reasons' would depend upon what we were valuing the picture as. We are now in a position to fill in this gap. To appreciate a painting as a work of art requires (at least) that we value it intrinsically and as irreplaceable.

This way of putting things has implications in two directions: it gives a suggestion about ways of valuing a painting which will not constitute valuing it as a work of art. This will take up the next chapter. It also encourages us to go on and see if we can be more specific about what the intrinsic and irreplaceable merits of particular paintings might be. This is the task of Chapters 4 and 5.

In this chapter a special kind of valuing (valuing something intrinsically and as irreplaceable) has been described. In a polemical vein, I would claim that this kind of valuing is more important than the whole discussion of the nature of art – of whether something is or is not to be called a work of art. It is not whether something belongs to the category 'art' but whether it is significantly valuable in the way described which really matters. There is no doubt, either, that it was this category of value to which all the great artists of the past took their work to belong. We cannot stop this category of value being central to us, but we may find that the cultural institution of the Artworld provides us with less and less that matters. It remains open, however, and always will, for someone to take up his brushes and paint works which are valuable in the way described; and their value is utterly independent of whether or not they are labelled 'art'.

The sortal phrase 'as a work of art' has been understood in a specific way which draws on intrinsic merit, irreplaceability and artistry. When understood in this way it picks out the relevant category of appreciation for the paintings in the National Gallery: it states the way in which they were intended to be appreciated. Given that the word 'art' has been used in a variety of ways, there is a variety of ways in which the phrase 'as a work of art' can be understood. However, I use the phrase only in the sense explained above. Thus I think that it matters that we appreciate paintings *as works of art* (that is, in respect of their intrinsic merits, irreplaceability and artistry) while I do not think that it matters very much whether an object is *called* 'art' (when this label is not used to signal intrinsic merit, irreplaceability and artistry).

Notes

1. When the surface quality of a work deteriorates with age we are no longer able to appreciate fully the artistic merits it had. This is not to say that changes are always for the worse. Raphael's *Madonna of the Pinks* (plate 3) now has some cracks visible on the painted surface. There is a way in which these cracks may add to our aesthetic enjoyment of the object: they lend the picture a tremendous poignancy. However, in being delighted by the cracks, one is not *thereby* appreciating Raphael's work of art.

2. There can be aesthetic qualities which we dislike. A feature of a work might be garish or clumsy, but to call that feature 'garish' or 'clumsy' is to imply that one has had an unpleasant perceptual experience of that feature. Thus, when a work is held in low esteem *as a work of art* is so on the basis of its aesthetic properties; for there are aesthetic properties which contribute to the failure of a work as a work of art.

It might be thought that these aesthetic features are highly subjective, peculiar to individual spectators. And it may further be held that such experiences cannot support generally valid judgments about artistic merit. The complexities of this discussion cannot be taken up here, although they are treated in the Appendix. Let me just note a couple of points here which are argued for there. First, it is not obvious that because a feature is recognised on the basis of an individual's experience, no generally valid judgment can be derived form it. Secondly, there are adequate grounds for taking certain perceptual responses to paintings as standard. One is entitled, with a high degree of intellectual respectability, to hold to the claim that judgments of artistic merit, which are based in part upon the experience of aesthetic features, are universally valid.

3. It is important to add that in valuing a picture as a work of art we need not value it *exclusively* for its aesthetic properties. Some have advocated the latter, and it is roughly definitional of 'Aestheticism'. However, no satisfactory argument for limiting the appreciation of a painting as a work of art to a concern with its aesthetic properties has ever been presented. It is, to say the least, evident that the creators of many great works were very concerned that we should appreciate other features too.

4. All that has been argued here is that the work is irreplaceable with respect to its visible properties. This leaves open the possibility that another object, perhaps a copy, with the same visible features would have the same artistic value. This would be true only if the artistic merit of a work depended upon its visible properties alone. The copy does not share other non-visible properties with the original. The complexities which surround the discussion of the artistic merit of copies cannot be adequately treated here.

3

Valuing a Painting as a
Work of Art

1. Guillotine

The seventeenth-century Dutch landscapes are on show at the rear of the National Gallery. A crowd has formed in front of Hobbema's celebrated *Avenue at Middelharnis* (plate 2).

'There is a story about Hobbema,' the guide tells us. 'He was a well established painter when in 1668 he got married to the maid of the Burgomaster of Amsterdam. By a series of backstairs wrangles he obtained a minor but lucrative post in the Excise: his job involved checking the quality of the wine imported into Amsterdam. Hobbema gave up painting when he got the job and this picture of Middelharnis was his final masterpiece.'

There is a pause while we savour Hobbema's career. 'But,' the guide continues 'the story isn't true. In fact, Hobbema painted this picture in 1689, twenty years after he took the wine-gauging job. He never gave up painting at all. The story, and the fact that the story caught on, reflects a will to romanticise the lives of painters.'

However interesting all this is, it does nothing to explain why this work by Hobbema is of high artistic merit, why it is a masterpiece. No amount of insight into the psychology of gossip is going to illuminate this issue.

'Why is this picture so well known?' The guide proceeds

to answer the question. 'This picture belonged to Sir Robert Peel, prime minister and picture collector. It passed into the National Gallery in 1871. This provenance has made the work quite exceptionally famous.' This is all very well, but it still says nothing about the artistic *merit* of the work: we know that fame is not the same thing as excellence. It is conceivable (just) that someone should be caused to admire the picture simply because it was in Peel's collection. We can imagine someone mad with snobbery who cannot help admiring everything connected with Peel, we can even imagine that this person is unaware of his own sycophancy. There is a great gulf between being caused to like a work (as the sycophant is) and having good reasons for admiring it as a work of art. It is perfectly true that some works do gain prominence on non-artistic grounds. But when all that is settled, we can still ask the question 'Is it any good as a work of art?' Nothing about the public prominence of the work will help us answer that question.

'The picture shows us some pleasant South Holland fields, carefully tended and intensively farmed. Although one gardener is shown on the right pruning a small tree, there is little evidence of the labour, the manual labour, which was actually required to produce this state of affairs. The picture suppresses a part of economic reality in order to present a more satisfying vision of farming life (more satisfying, that is, to the land-owning class). This picture was almost certainly commissioned by the Kruislander family who owned market gardens in the region.'

So, it is revealed, the work is interesting as an index of the preferences of certain people in the seventeenth century. This makes it valuable as a document in political and social history. Again this is beside the point when we are concerned with appreciating the picture as a work of art. A painting does not succeed or fail as a work of art simply upon the basis of the niceness of the political attitudes which can be read into it, or the information it yields about times past.

'Look at the avenue, it was cut down a few years after the picture was painted. The high-roofed barn on the right, which was used for drying *meekrap*, was pulled down in about 1880 after the sudden collapse of the *meekrap* market. The church tower is still standing although the spire was removed in 1811. The spire had to go to make room for a semaphore: Middelharnis was one of the links in the semaphore chain from Amsterdam to Paris.'

It is clear that such comments would apply to any relatively competent picture of that scene done around that time. So, no matter how interested we are in historical geography, this on its own gives us no grounds for valuing the picture as irreplaceable. If we just want to see something of how the actual scene looked that year then any old painting would do just as well.

The notion of artistic merit which was advanced in Chapter 2 (concerning the intrinsic value and irreplaceable features of the work) acts as a guillotine ruling out some ways of attending to the picture as irrelevant to appreciating it as a work of art. A kind of value has been elucidated, and there are ways of being interested in pictures which do not connect with valuing them in *that* way.

'The painter has arranged the avenue of trees with great care. Trace down the surface of the canvas the lines made by the tops of the trees, see how they gradually come together and meet at the horizon. Follow the same line further and note how they pick up in the edges of the path. We can attend to the X figure which these lines form on the painted surface. In the *depicted* space, of course, these lines are parallel: the sides of the path are parallel, the tops of the trees are (roughly) parallel. We can see the picture as structured in two ways at once: in two dimensions (the X figure) and in the represented three dimensions.'

'Surely this will satisfy even the most cantankerous in the audience,' the guide thinks to himself. But what he has said still does not give us grounds for esteeming this picture as a masterpiece. The same phenomenon (lines running parallel into represented space and forming an X on the material surface) could be instantiated in many pictures, and in pictures of mediocre or low artistic value. So the guillotine falls, too, on this offering.

Nevertheless it would be churlish to pretend that the last feature is not relevant to the picture's artistic merit. For it is not too hard to enrich the description of this feature so that it gives us a reason for valuing this picture uniquely. We can attend to the particular X shape which has been formed by Hobbema, and we can attend to the particular way in which he has represented parallel tree tops and road sides. He has instituted a certain irregularity into the figure and succeeds in representing the trees and road in an apparently *uncontrived* way, while presenting them in a bold and highly *contrived* surface pattern. Another painter could not render this feature in *the same way* as Hobbema, without thereby reproducing a large portion of Hobbema's picture.

In passing let me point out that the feature we are discussing cannot be understood in merely formal terms. If we consider 'form' to be just the surface patterns, then the contrast between surface pattern and represented objects disappears. If we extend 'form' to include the shape of represented objects, then we have to take into account the objects represented. And in doing so our approach to the picture is not purely 'formalist'. One can only describe the recession and parallel lines in the picture with reference to what is depicted.

We can now see what the guide should concentrate on if he is concerned about the picture as a work of art. He should concentrate on the particular way in which the content of the work is rendered in paint by the artist.

2. Artistry

A difficulty has so far been kept on the sidelines: the notion of intrinsic value rather *under-describes* what it is that a painting offers the appreciative eye. Take the difference between looking at a beautiful tree and looking at a fine painting of a tree. Both are experiences of intrinsic value, so the difference between these experiences cannot be explained simply in terms of intrinsic value. A cedar of Lebanon, with its lovely spread of grey-green leaves in high summer, set off against the warmer tones of the bark and the limpid evening sky beyond, has great intrinsic value. Yet there is an important difference in the way the tree is valuable and the way in which a picture of a tree is valuable.

The picture displays artistry while the tree does not. We appreciate the way the resources of the art-form have been used by the painter in the achievement of intrinsic value; there is no equivalent of this in the appreciation of the tree. But what exactly is artistry?

Let us start by looking at an example: the *Tree Study* (plate 4) once attributed to Claude and more recently to Poussin. Someone might praise this work for the accuracy of its drawing: the artist manages to present a likeness of the tree. Now, it is perfectly possible for someone to be superbly good at drawing trees and yet never produce a work of stature. The ability to so depict does not explain the artist's ability to produce fine work. In one sense, accurate depiction is an artistic sub-ability. If the painter had not been able to depict accurately, he would not have been able to produce this tree study. However, this ability (to produce an accurate depiction) on its own does not explain how he was able to produce a fine as opposed to a mediocre tree study. As it stands, the exercise of this ability does not count as an exercise of artistry on the artist's part.

A further ability which the artist exercises is that of balancing the demands of accuracy of depiction and gracefulness of design so that he produces a graceful, accurate representation (a graceful representation which is beautiful). This ability cannot be broken into two capacities: for accuracy of depiction and for harmonious arrangement of the surface of the picture. This two-step procedure would not reliably produce the outcome, and so we must attribute to the artist another ability not reducible to the conjunction of those two: namely, the ability to make a gracefully disposed accurate drawing of a tree. For this, the ability to draw accurately, just as the ability to design the surface, is necessary but not sufficient. And although both are necessary they are not jointly sufficient.

The feature which the picture has as a result of the successful exercise of this capacity is that of being a well disposed accurate depiction. This precise feature is one which can be valued intrinsically and irreplaceably. For no other feature could be accurate and well-disposed *in the same way* and not look the same as the feature referred to.

One central success of this picture is the way in which the marks on the paper succeed in doing more than one thing at a time. Take, for example, the marks which depict the bough on the right-hand side. Imagine the artist applying the ink and wash. The marks produced achieve a number of things at once. (a) They form a graceful pattern themselves; (b) they cohere with the pattern of the whole; (c) they proceed from observation, resembling the characteristic curves of a bough; (d) they bound the right-hand side of the pictured space, effectively containing the rich variety of the central tree and its foliage, not letting the eye stray off the edge of the paper; (e) they help create a planar perspective so that the central tree seems firmly located in space at a definite distance from the represented point of view; (f) they succeed in terms of colour as well as outline, and also in tone and in the density of the wash; (g) they create the impression of sunlight beyond, (h) they look as if they have been applied easily and lightly; (i) they achieve all this while not detracting from the central object depicted. Artistry is the ability to kill many birds with one stone.

3. Imagination

It seems clear that a work could involve a very great deal of artistry and yet not have a high value as a work of art. This entails that artistic value cannot simply be determined by the degree of artistry exhibited. Artistry is not the only thing which counts towards the value of a picture as a work of art. There are many factors relevant to artistic value which have little to do with the artist's skill. The truth of asserted content may matter for the value of the work: it may matter for the value of contemplating the work. There are certain eighteenth-century erotic etchings which involve great artistic skill in the handling of detail and the expression of the situation's erotic character. Yet this work may properly be judged not to be of high artistic value, because the experience it invites the spectator to enjoy is not one of high value: from the point of view of intrinsic merit and considered as irreplaceable, what the picture offers is not of high value.

There is, too, another quality which a painter requires apart from artistry if work of stature is to be produced. If we think about a field well apart from painting the point is easily made – the football field, for instance. A player can have considerable artistry in his control of the ball and the grace with which he carries out various manoeuvres.

The problem is that he has no imagination: it never occurs to him to carry out anything but routine manoeuvres. A positive description of the way in which a painting can be imaginative requires us to dwell on particular examples, and this is a pleasure which will have to be deferred (to Chapter 5). The point of mentioning imagination here is to make vivid the claim that artistry is not on its own sufficient for artistic excellence even though it is a central strand.

Artistry and imagination are the *abilities* characteristic of the production of works of art, without being the unique determinants of artistic value. The exercise of artistry and imagination is *not sufficient* for the creation of a work of high artistic merit, although the exercise of artistry and imagination is a *necessary* condition for high artistic value. Among the most resonant words of criticism are 'very well done; not worth doing in the first place'. One may execute a feeble conception with great artistry; it remains, all the same, a feeble conception, and the very beguiling quality of the artistry is lamentable, for it makes something trivial more attractive than it deserves to be. Artistry and imagination can serve trumpery wares just as much as they can be necessary for the realisation of a profound work.[1]

4. Lessing

Appreciation, it has been claimed in Chapter 1, involves valuing the work *for the right reasons*. Concern with intrinsic value brings down the guillotine on a number of responses to paintings which simply cannot count as the appreciation of those paintings as works of art. A number of possible responses have been shown to have nothing to do with the appreciation of the work: liking a painting merely for its historical content has nothing to do with grasping the intrinsic value of the picture – the picture is treated merely as a vehicle for the communication of information which could perfectly well have been communicated in some other way. The emphasis has been on cases of *failure* to appreciate; nothing has been said about what the 'right reasons' for liking the painting, and thereby appreciating its intrinsic value, might be.

One of the enduring fantasies of intellectual ambition has been the hope that *from the very idea of art itself* could be *deduced* the qualities which would make successful works of art. The most elaborate example of this was provided by Gotthold Lessing, the eighteenth-century German dramatist and critic. Starting with the idea that all art must represent dramatic action *beautifully*, Lessing arrived at fantastically specific conclusions: in sculpture the principal figures must be naked, they must not be open-mouthed, and their wrists must be clearly represented. The problem with this procedure is clear: only from a very elaborate set of starting assumptions can conclusions such as these be drawn, but it is the very elaborateness of the starting assumptions which makes them unconvincing. The only reason Lessing was able to draw such exotic rabbits out of his hat was that he had carefully put them there in the first place. From a minimal suggestion about art, namely that paintings, drawings and so on characteristically serve intrinsic value, it cannot be hoped that elaborate conclusions about artistic excellence will easily follow. If the hat really is empty we cannot expect to be able to draw any rabbits out of it.

Rather than dictate what the good qualities of a picture must be (like Lessing) the following three chapters look at specific pictures in an attempt to understand how painters have used the resources of the art form to create intrinsic value. The study of artistry is an *empirical* study: it relies upon the observation of what painters actually do in the creation of works which have intrinsic value.

It is not surprising that the two questions: 'How does

the intrinsic value of a painting differ from that of, say, a beautiful tree?' and 'How does the painter *create* intrinsic value?' should fall together. It is precisely the fact *that it is painted* which makes the picture valuable in subtly different ways from other lovely or fine things.

Notes

1. This point gives a way of responding to one of the established conundrums of criticism. Some paintings were painted with repellent aims in mind, such as propaganda pictures which promote appalling causes. It is perfectly possible that such work should display a high degree of artistry (in the sense spelled out in the preceding section). We can judge the artistry quite apart from the moral judgment about the ends to which it was put; but in evaluating the work as a whole there is no reason why we should ignore its repellent purpose. The work, taken as a whole, does not have a high intrinsic value, on the contrary it has a large negative intrinsic value.

4

Resources of Painting

1. Bread and paint

'Is it not strange,' someone in Shakespeare says, 'that sheep guts should hale souls out of men's bodies.' With such unpromising resources – vibrating sheep gut, wood and horsehair – are produced passages of sublime music. Suppose someone said, merely, that he was going to make sheep gut vibrate and arrange the sounds in time, no great future would be predicted for this activity. But, in one sense, Beethoven's late Quartets are no more than sounds arranged in time. So it is with painting: from the mere act of mixing pigment in oil or water and applying it to a wall or canvas no one could predict what Michelangelo or Titian were able to do, or that paintings would come to occupy such a privileged and highly regarded position in our culture. How comes so much from so little?

Imagine a sort of historical-prediction multiple-choice question: 'Which of the following is most likely to produce objects which are regarded across generations as touchstones of value?

(1) Mixing flour, yeast, and water and heating them up.
(2) Throwing stones in ponds.
(3) Arranging smells in time.
(4) Putting colours on bits of cloth.'

We know now that much more has been done with the last

than with the others, but this would not be in any way obvious from the question. What is it about painting, about putting colour on cloth, which has enabled so much to be done with it?

Philosophical discussions get strung out across the years, which is why philosophers are often not very good conversationalists: they are used to waiting a long time before giving their replies. Kant's brilliant replies to Hume (famous for asking difficult questions) could not have impressed the admirable Scotsman, coming as they did five years after his death, and indeed forty-two years after he posed them. But in the history of philosophy this counts as quick-fire repartee. This chapter is conceived as a reply to an adolescent worry (the years of adolescence have now definitively replaced the muses as the source of creative endeavour). I had been parading my attachment to painting before my elder cousin when with a sudden weariness he turned on me: 'Oh, painting! It's just an accident that it's painting that gets all the attention, it could just as well have been baking bread or arranging flowers that had all this emotion and meaning invested in it.'

There is nothing special, I took him to be saying, about the act of putting colours on canvas which makes it more suited than other activities (such as baking bread or flower arranging) to the creation of captivating or profound works.

The way would then lie open for alternative explanations of the cultural prominence of painting: perhaps it receives attention because it was adopted by aristocratic leaders of fashion (it was, from the Renaissance on, a delicate accomplishment, whereas baking never was); perhaps painting was a man's activity and so was considered more important than flower arranging, a woman's occupation and therefore to be relegated to the second division. 'There is nothing special about painting itself,' they say, 'only external factors, like who did it, came to give it a cultural prominence over some other interesting activities.' That we take painting to be important is what is to be explained. But this deflationary line only comes into play if we *cannot* find a reply which shows that (after all) there *are* things about putting paint on canvas which explain its cultural significance. At the time I could think of nothing very clever to say in reply to my cousin, but if he is still interested this and the next chapter are my answer.

The central point in this delayed response is a simple one: painting presents the artist with an especially rich set of resources for the creation of intrinsic value. This is not to say that making bread or arranging flowers are activities entirely lacking in such potential, but (with all due respect) only rather meagre resources have been uncovered. Between the minimal descriptions of putting colours on a support, and of mixing flour, yeast and water and heating it, there is little to choose. But over the centuries of experimentation and refinement it has emerged that an enormous amount can be done with painting. Its depths of resource, its subtle openings of opportunity, have been discovered (if not exhaustively mapped). By contrast nothing of the kind has emerged when it comes to making bread. No matter how delicious and wholesome, a loaf of bread doesn't mean anything very much. This is not an accidental feature, a sign of our lack of respect for the trade of baking bread. Rather, it indicates the restricted resources bread offers. No opportunities emerge for the baker to impress the loaf with the imprint of his deepest emotions, to make it answer to his joys and troubles or to convey visions and denunciations.

This chapter sets out some of the resources which pigment, oil and canvas offer the painter and some of the opportunities they afford for the exercise of artistry. The way to find out about this is to look carefully at paintings and at what painters have made use of in painting.

2. Figures in the medium

We go into the National Gallery in Trafalgar Square, sailing through a succession of rooms filled with tempting objects, but we hold our course until we come to a stop before the *View from Louveciennes* (plate 8) by Camille Pissarro. What do we see? Two descriptions come quickly to mind. We might say that we see a rough country lane, a woman in a bonnet walking away from us, some trees coming into blossom and so on. While this reaction comes very easily, there is something amiss with it. When we look at Pissarro's picture, the road is streaked with paint, the trees have branches made of sinuous, intermittent lines, there are smudges where the sky meets the distant trees. This is not normally the case when we see the sky or a road.

A second reaction we might have had to the question: 'What do you see?' is as follows. Supposing we go very close: a pattern of coloured marks strikes the eye, and one is intently aware that the painting is an expanse of coloured shapes. Yet this does not really describe how the painting normally looks to us – it does no justice to the urge we have to describe the painting in terms of trees, clouds, people, road and blossom. A more accurate description of how this painting *looks* has to accommodate both of these answers: the answer in terms of subject matter and the answer in terms of paint. The right description has to take account both of what is depicted and of the medium in which it is depicted. We see a painted sky, a painted road, painted blossom.

On looking at the picture, the spectator does not first see the cloud and then notice the paint. Nor do we first see the paint and then piece it together as a depiction of a cloud. We see painted clouds, or paint used to depict clouds.

Take a very familiar example: the stick man. When you look at a drawing of a stick man, you do not *first* see the lines and *then* see them as representing a man. You see them straight away as lines which depict a man. You do not have the impression of seeing a man and only then notice that in fact it is a set of lines you are looking at. The proper description of our visual experience in front of the *View from Louveciennes* requires mention of both elements: our awareness of the medium: the paint; and our awareness of what the medium is being used to depict: clouds. The question arises what can a painter do with this resource: the fact that when we look at a painting we can see the subject matter formulated in the medium?

3. Depiction

One major possibility which depiction opens up is that of determinate content of a special sort: namely visual content. A great part of our most intense experience is fundamentally visual in character. It is so much so that description provides only a secondary access and reference to those experiences. The painting may recapture and preserve what is intense, fleeting and valuable in perception. And in so doing, it preserves the tender or serious emotion which was bound up with the perception. Our visual perceptions are often intimately engaged with feeling such that a full characterisation of the experience requires reference both to what is seen and to what is felt. Literature provides testament to such intimate ties and examples of certain moments of experience in which sight and feeling are inextricably entwined.

Such is the following description from Proust. The narrator remembers walking as a child along the banks of the Vivonne.

Suddenly a roof, a gleam of sunlight on a stone, the smell of a path would make me stop still, to enjoy the special pleasure that each of them gave me, and also because they appeared to be concealing, beyond what my eyes could see, something which they invited me to come and take but which despite all my efforts I never managed to discover … . I would concentrate on recalling exactly the line of the roof, the colour of the stone, which, without my being able to understand why, had seemed to me to be bursting, ready to open, to yield up to me the secret treasure of which they were themselves no more than the lids.[1]

Dostoevsky recounts the passionate final regard of a man who thinks he is about to be shot:

A church stood not far off and its gilded roof sparkled in the sunshine. He remembered staring with an awful intensity at the roof; he couldn't drag his eyes away; it occurred to him that those rays were his new state of being, and that in three minutes he would somehow merge with them …[2]

The depiction allows the painter not merely to report what a stone or church roof looked like, but to recapture something of the intensity of the experience, the experience in which the gleam of sunlight on a stone seemed full of mysterious significance, or in which the prisoner could not drag his eyes away from the church roof. The thing is, of course, not just to recapture any old experience, but certain experiences which stand out as important. Clearly, merely to copy a stone or a roof would not suffice to recapture those moments. The possibility of depiction is a necessary condition for preserving the visual experience. Music or literature or abstract painting might evoke the feelings, but they cannot reproduce the experience as visual.

Perhaps no single feature has done more than the resource of depiction to explain how painting has come to be so culturally significant, because depiction establishes an intimate link to visual perception. Paint on canvas can be used to reproduce and to preserve visual experience at its most intense and serious moments; it is not surprising that something which can do this has become important.

But mere reportage, however interesting, can yield no artistic value, that is, can give a painting no intrinsic value. For reporting and recording are functions which, in principle, can always be accomplished by other means, by other, different pictures. Yet no painting does present the viewer with mere reportage, for always the subject matter has been painted. What happens is that, sometimes, scant attention is paid to the resources of painting, and the spectator is encouraged to look past the painting to its subject matter. In this and the next chapter I shall be considering depiction not in isolation, but the resource of depiction in conjunction with other resources of painting, examining the interplay of these and the value this interplay holds for the contemplative eye.

4. Use of the medium

Some pictures, and some styles of painting, make great play with the medium. Think, for example, of Cézanne's *Mountains in Provence* (plate 5). When we look at the distant hillside, the scoring of the brush is evident. The fields have faces depicted with patches of paint which clearly bear the traces of the strokes with which they were laid on. The outline of a field, if we look closely, has been formed both by the intention of rendering a field and by the physical quality of the paint as it was laid down with the brush.

What opportunities does the possibility of such a technique afford the artist? How might a painter exploit this resource? One thing it can be used for is to generate coherence in a work. Thus the fact that everything in a particular work is depicted in that way, with the precise work of the brush and the physical character of paint everywhere in evidence, lends the ensemble a layer of unity which it could not otherwise have. In Cézanne's painting, the distant fields and the foreground rocks equally bear the scored traces of the brush. This gives the fields-as-painted something in common with the rocks-as-painted. This common factor can exist only in painting. It is a common factor which cannot possibly exist between real fields and real rocks. The common factor of how they are painted goes some way to explaining the harmony of the picture.

It is not that Cézanne has emphasised a common feature between the fields and the rocks. We could imagine a painter noticing a common tone of fields and rocks which could be emphasised in the painting. This similarity does not require painting for its existence. By contrast, the similarity I have pointed to can only exist within painting.

The technique can also be used to lend emphatic differentiation to a part of the picture. Thinking back to Corot's oil sketch, *Avignon from the West* (plate 1), the sense of focus on the city in the distance is highly important. But how does Corot achieve a sense of focus? In part it is brought about by a transition from the foreground in which the application of the paint is loose and energetic and one is strongly aware of the medium. In this part of the painting, patches of colour are the shape they are in virtue of the flow and daub of paint and only loosely in response to the shape of the thing they depict. This is particularly evident when we look just to the right of the tree. Two dark areas, divided by a lighter patch, have become almost abstract, they swirl with the movement of paint, they lose contact with whatever it may be they depict: some trees, a road, the side of a hill, who can say precisely?

From this area the eye moves towards the city and the palace: there the strokes of the brush have been much more tightly controlled, and the traces of the brush marks themselves have been – for the most part – covered over. Great care has been taken in recording the visual accents of the buildings.

We have been discussing a purely artistic way of getting the eye to focus on the building: it exploits a resource which is only available in painting, namely a *contrast* in the way different parts of the picture have been painted, in terms of *how* paint has been used to depict objects.

This section has served to illustrate just two ways in which *how* objects are rendered in paint may be important for the elaboration of meaning in the picture. There are indefinitely many related devices. A swaggering figure can be depicted with swaggering brush strokes, a dissolute young man with flowing paint; in each case the way the figure is rendered adds to the spectator's experience of the depicted object.

5. Flatness and space

One feature of our visual experience of Pissarro's painting is so obvious that it is easy to overlook: we are aware of a flat opaque painted surface before us. 'But', comes the annoyed reply, 'I see the road running away from me, I see the trees in the distance, and yet you talk of a flat surface!' It is supposed that these two things cannot be compatible; all the same, they are. To see why, take a simpler example first. It is perfectly possible *at the same time* to see a line in a drawing as a line and also see that it depicts the slope of a cheek and the turn of the head. Our seeing the depiction of space does not in this case require that we lose sight of the flat qualities of the support and the fact that the medium is arranged on a flat surface. Admittedly, this is not true of all paintings, but it is true of many, and so

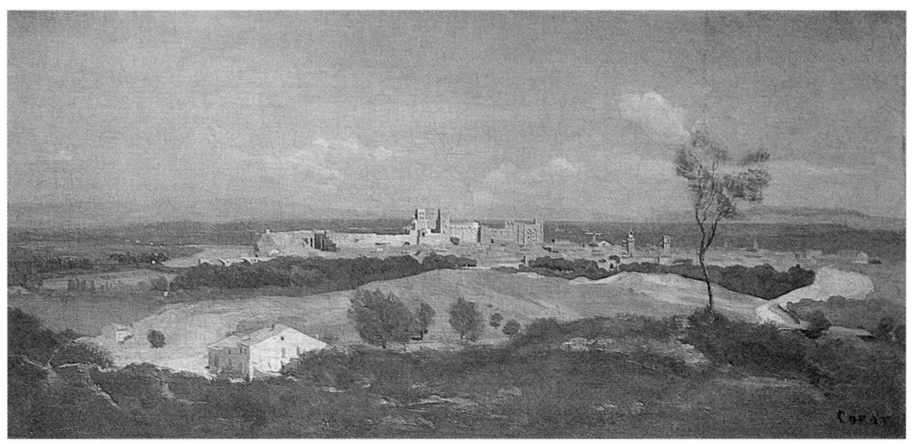

1. J.B.C. Corot: *Avignon from the West* (National Gallery, London)

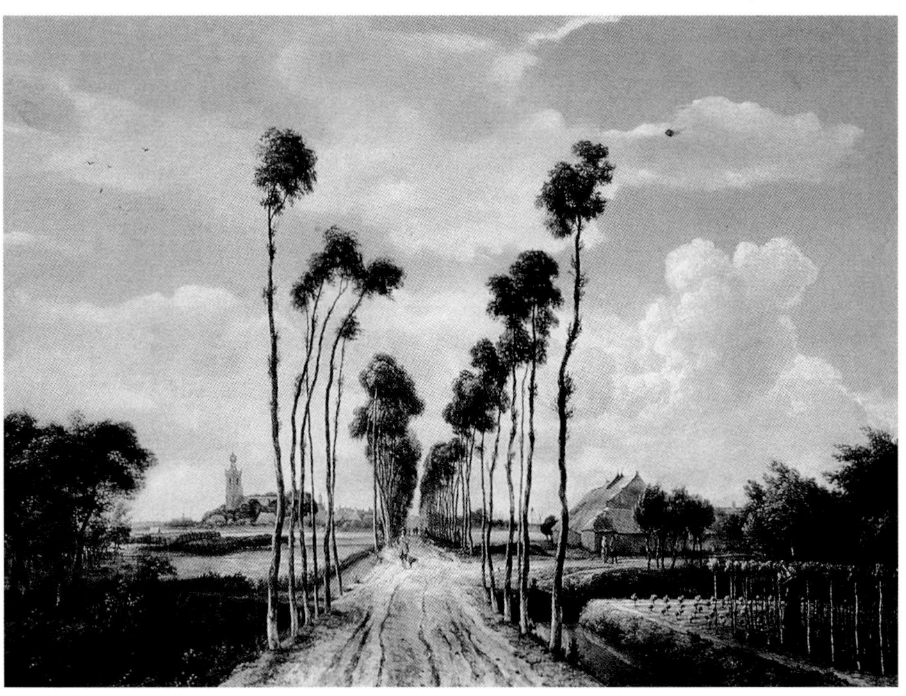

2. Meindert Hobbema: *The Avenue at Middelharnis* (National Gallery, London)

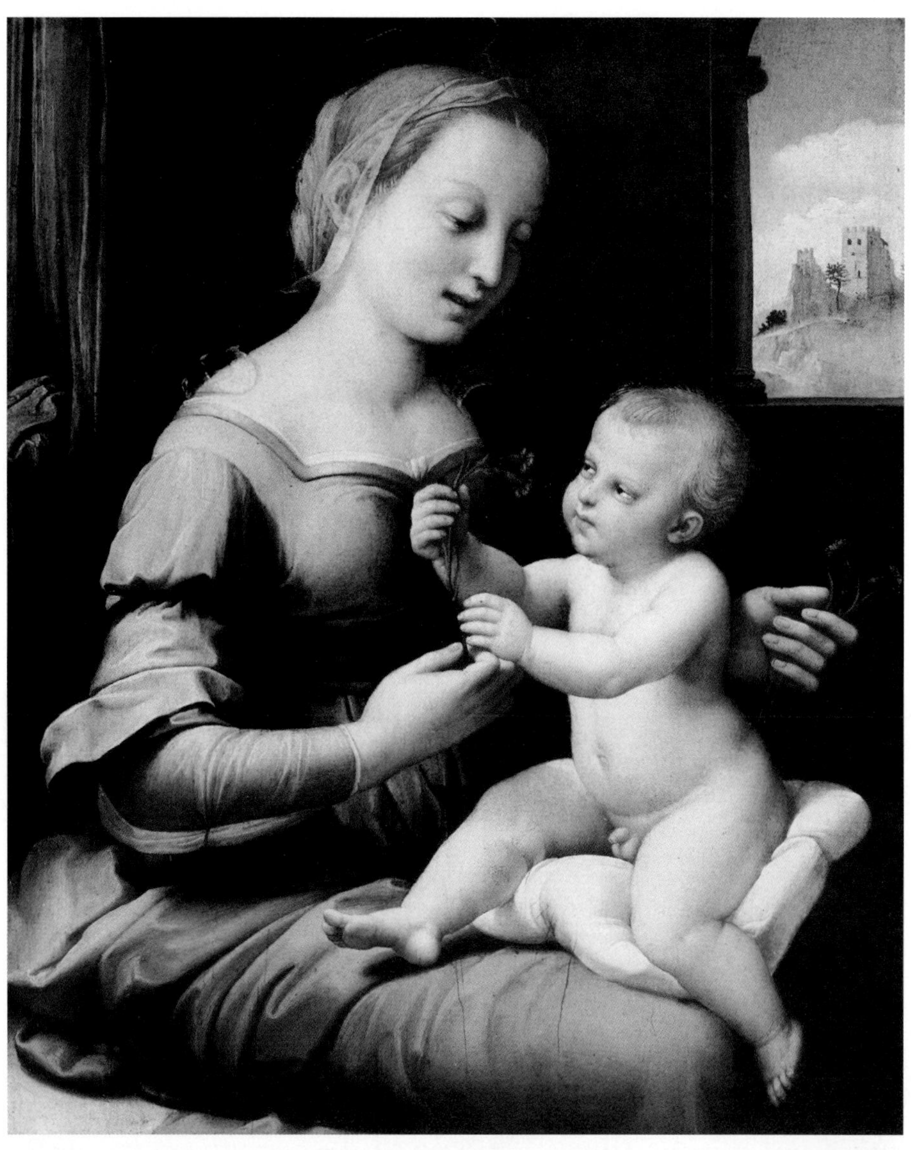

3. Raphael: *The Madonna of the Pinks* (National Gallery, London)

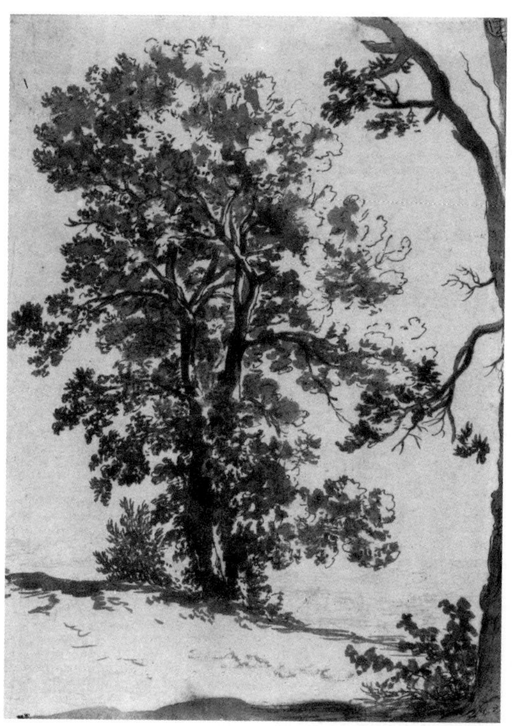

4. Nicolas Poussin: *Tree Study* (Louvre, Paris)

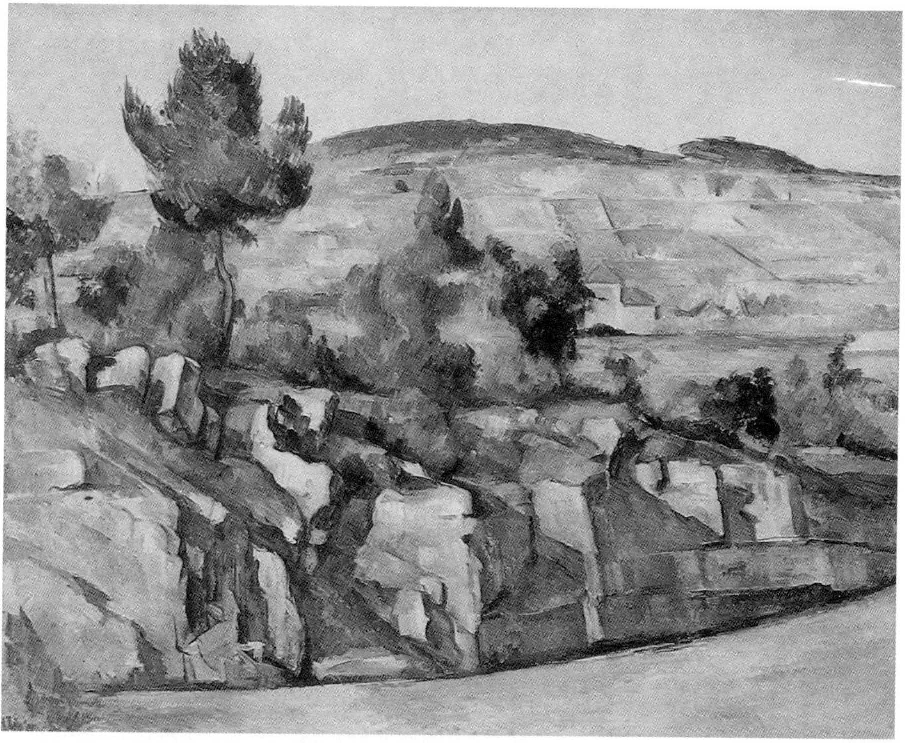

5. Paul Cézanne: *Mountains in Provence* (National Gallery, London)

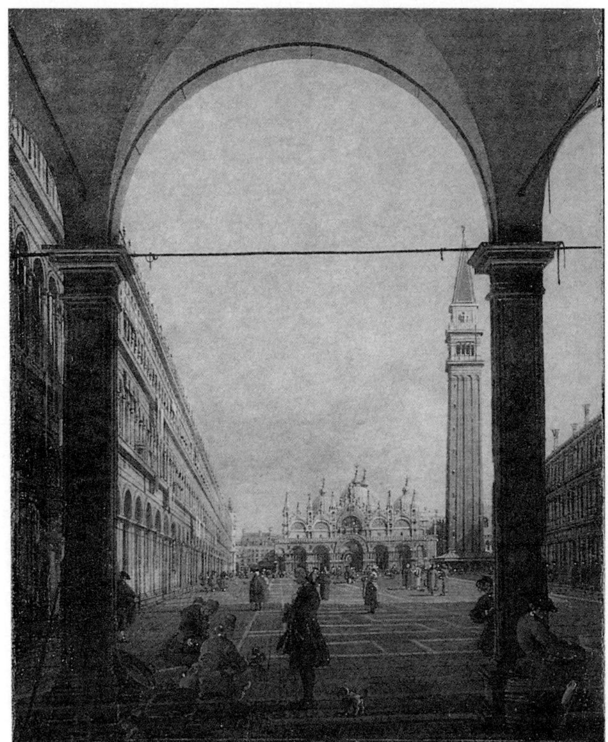

6. Canaletto: *Piazza San Marco dall'Ascensione* (National Gallery, London)

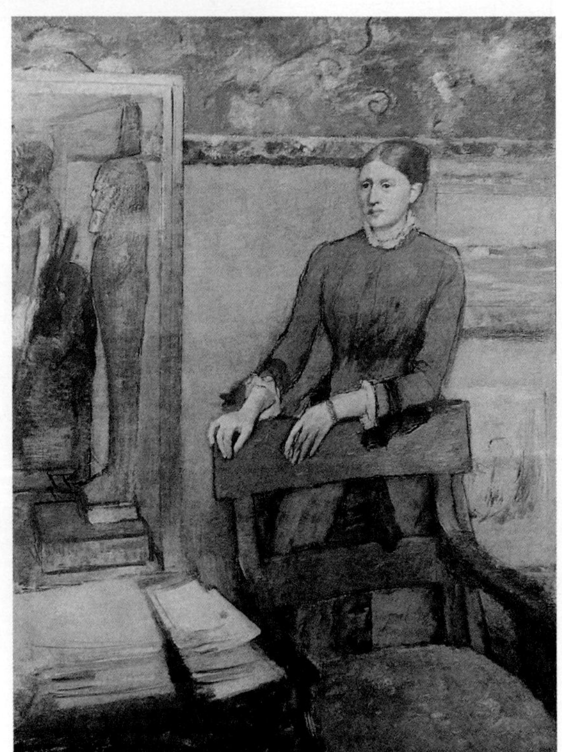

7. Edgar Degas: *Hélène Rouart in her Father's Study* (National Gallery, London)

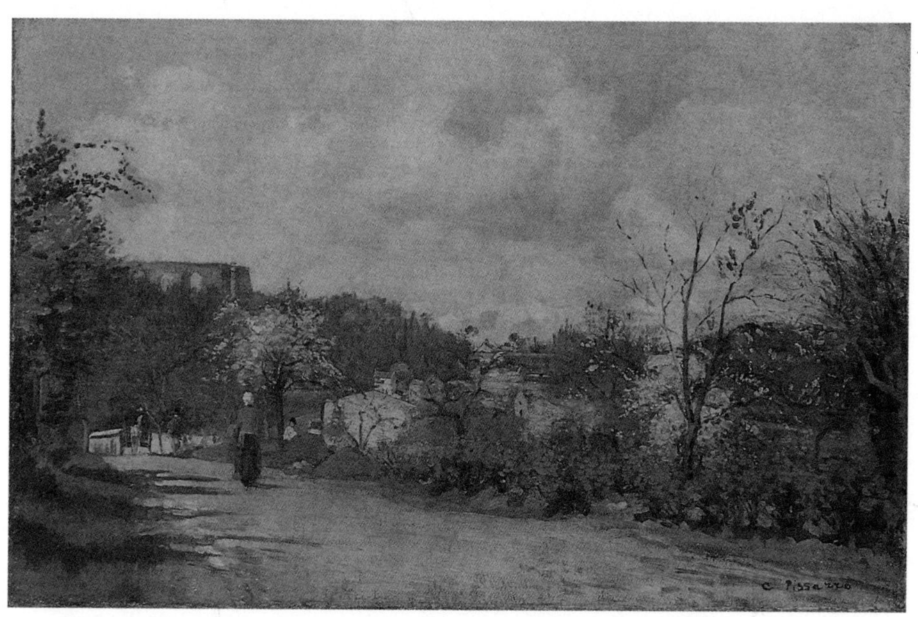

8. Camille Pissarro: *View from Louveciennes* (National Gallery, London)

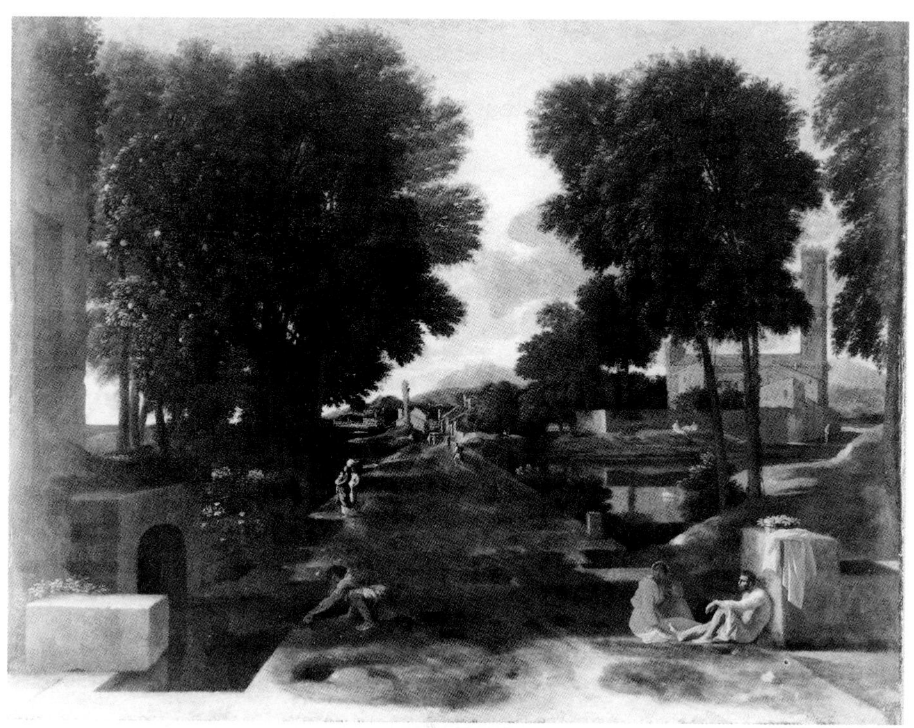

9. Nicolas Poussin: *A Roman Road* (Dulwich Picture Gallery, London)

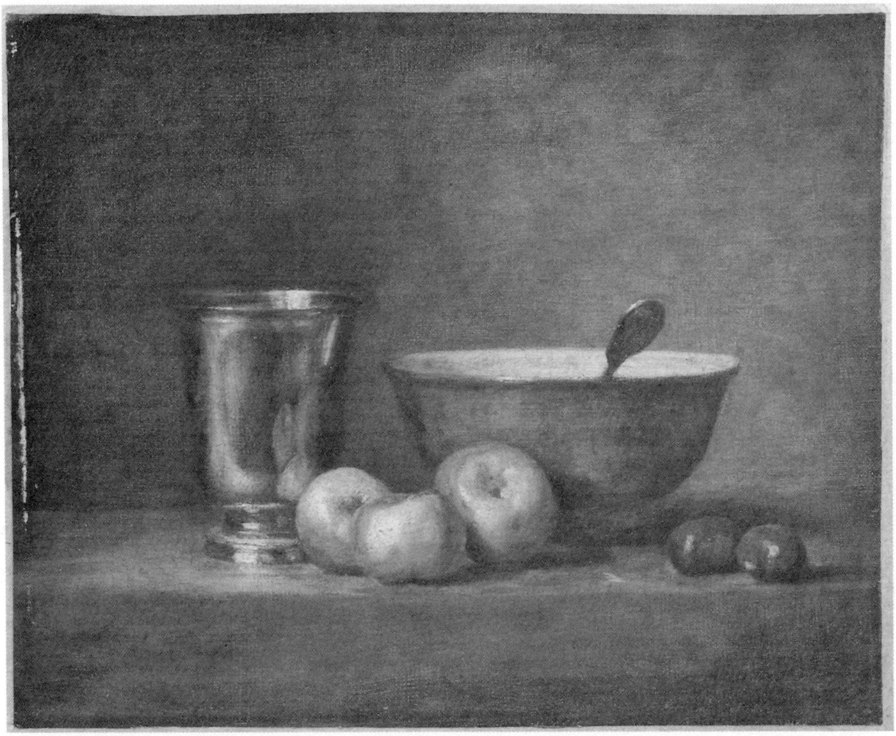

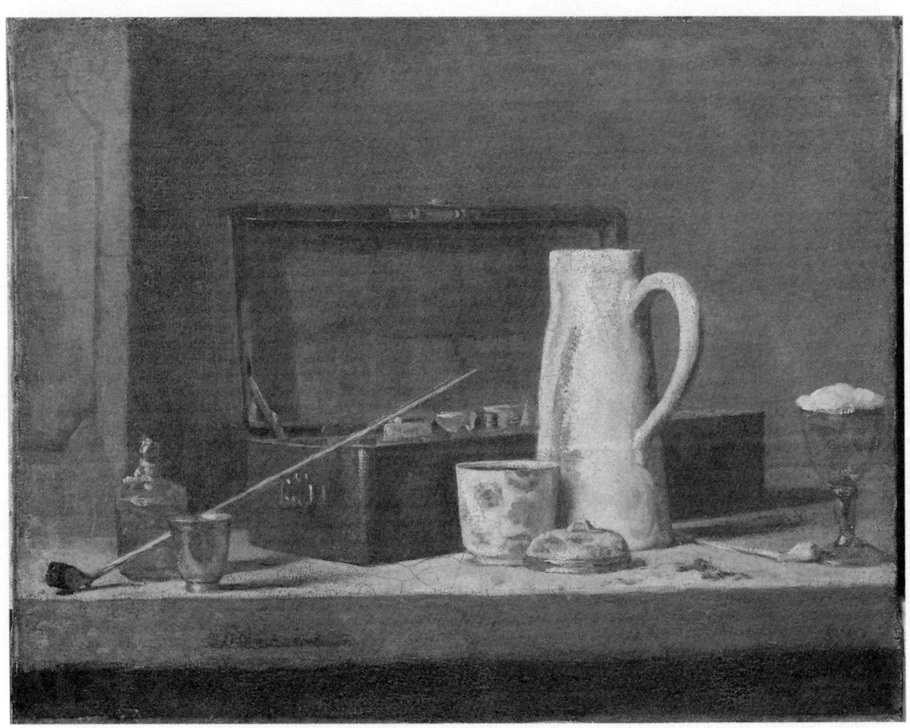

10. J.B. Chardin: *The Silver Goblet* (Louvre, Paris; © Photo RMN)

11. J.B. Chardin: *The Smoker's Case* (Louvre, Paris; © Photo RMN – Jean)

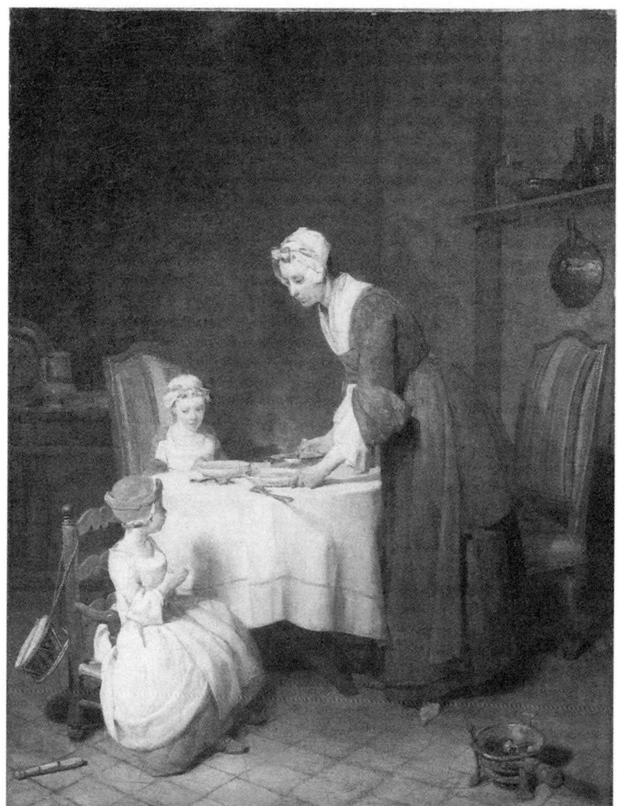

12. J.B. Chardin: *Saying Grace* (Louvre, Paris; © Photo RMN)

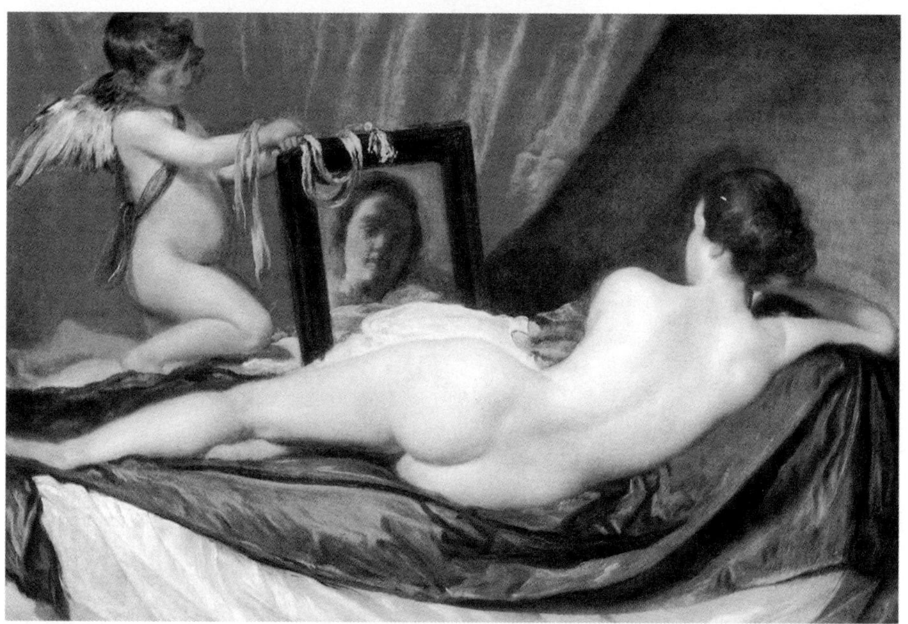

13. Diego de Silva y Velásquez: *The Rokeby Venus* (National Gallery, London)

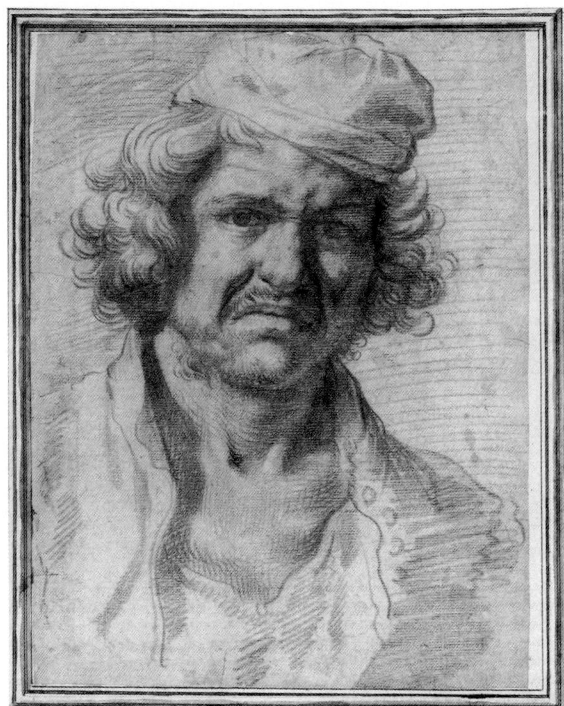

15. Raphael: *Studies for Two Apostles* (Ashmolean Museum, Oxford)

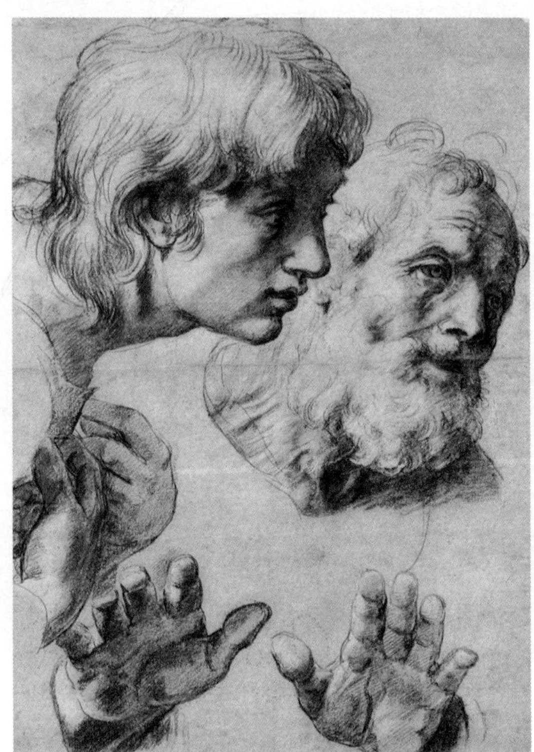

14. Nicolas Poussin: *Self Portrait* (British Museum, London)

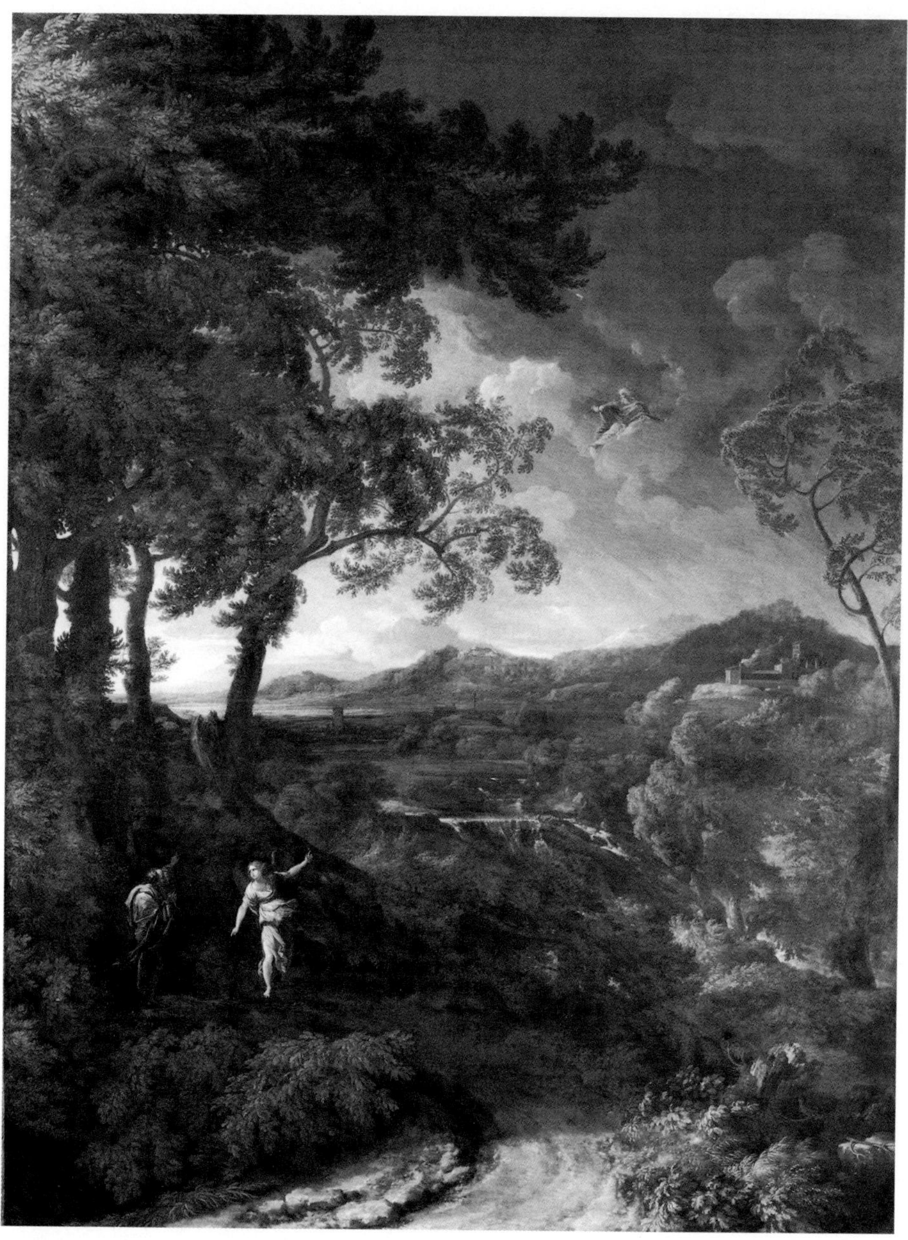

16. Gaspard Dughet: *Elijah with the Angel* (National Gallery, London)

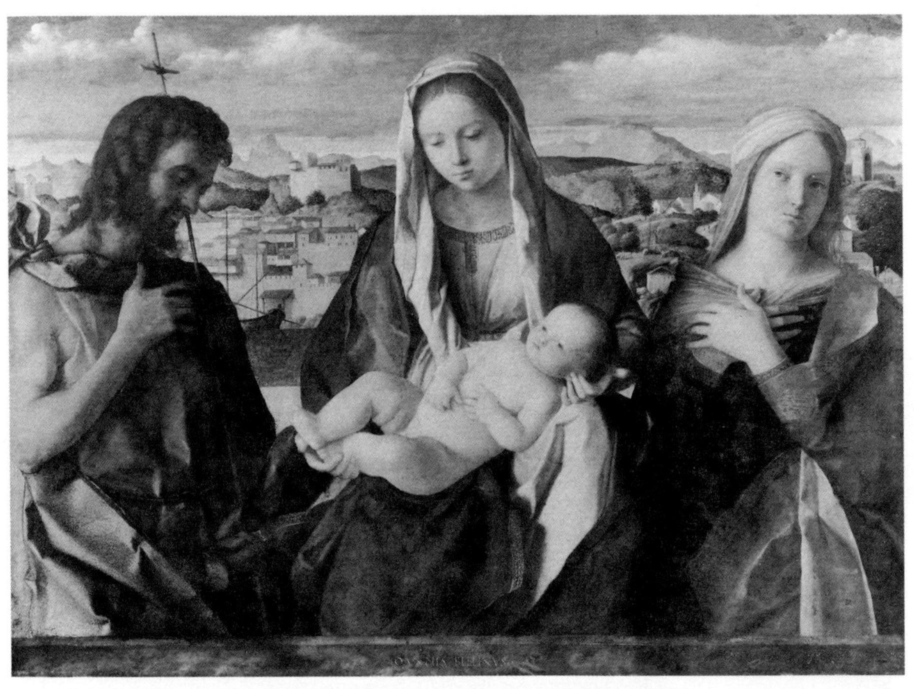

17. Giovanni Bellini: *Madonna* (Accademia, Venice; Photo Mansell Collection)

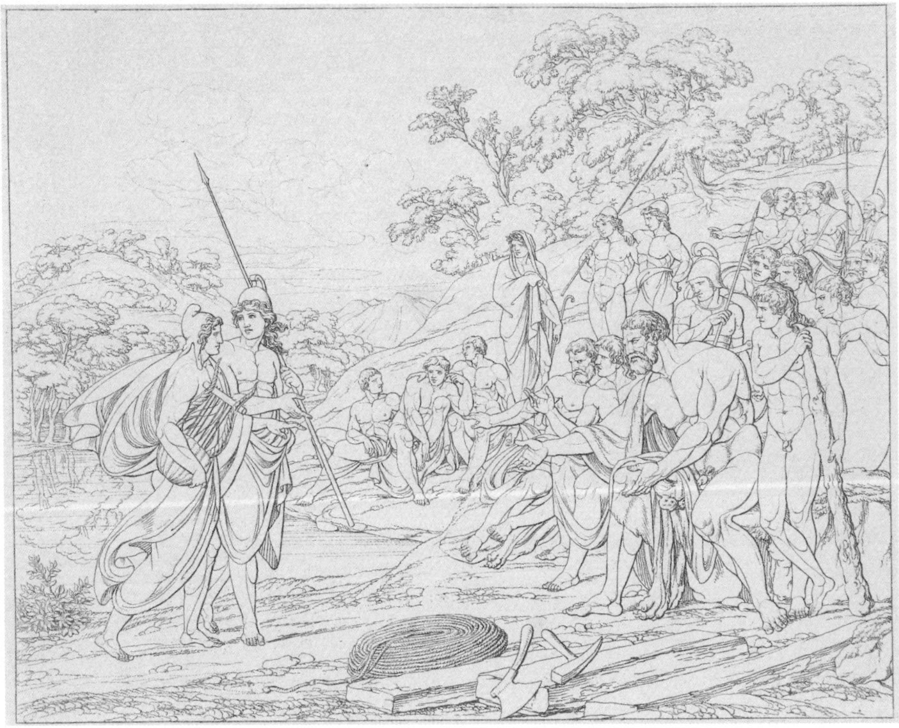

18. Koch: *Jason Presenting Orpheus to the Argonauts* (British Museum, London)

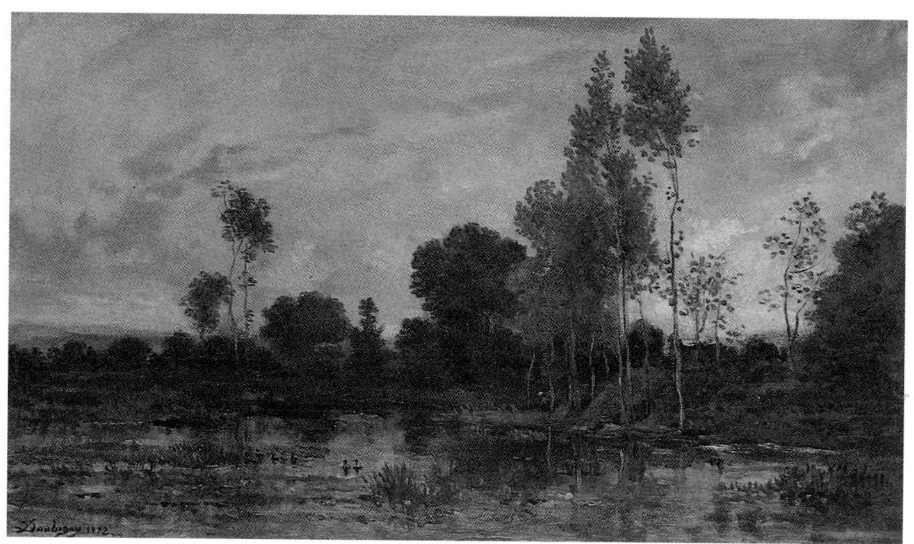

19. Charles Daubigny: *Alders* (National Gallery, London)

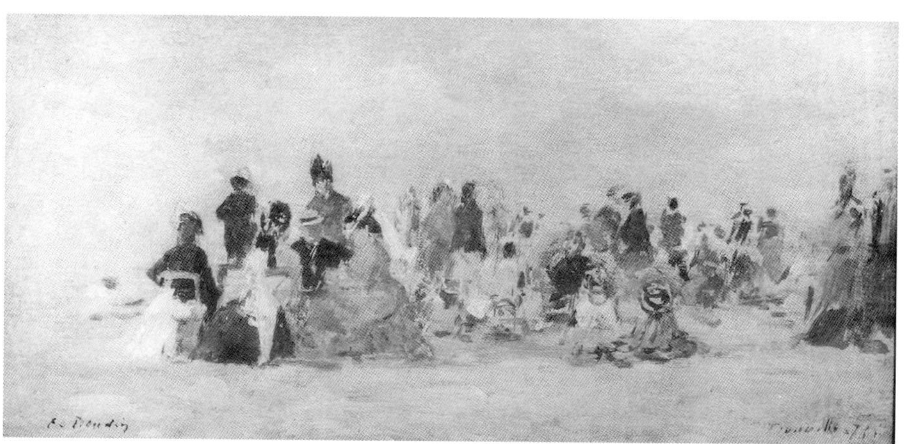

20. Eugène Boudin: *Trouville 1875* (Courtauld Institute Galleries, London)

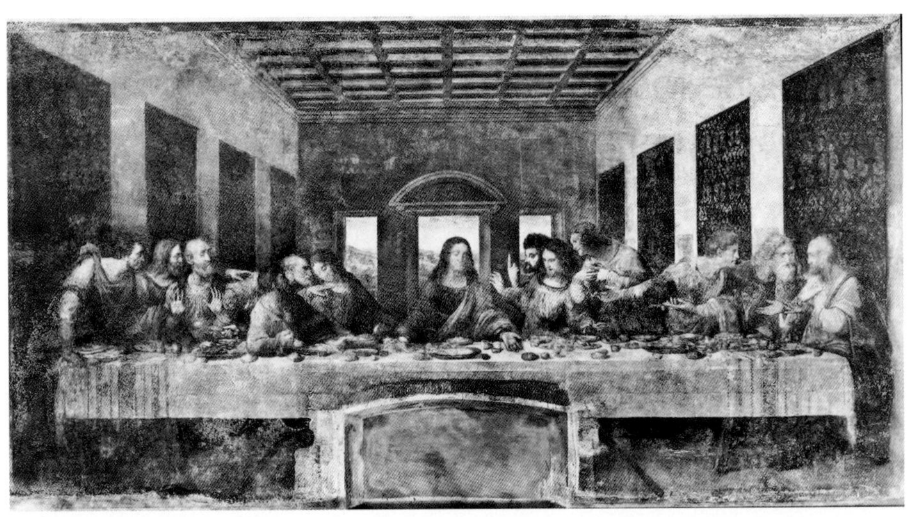

21. Leonardo da Vinci: *The Last Supper* (S. Maria della Grazie, Milan; Photo Mansell Collection)

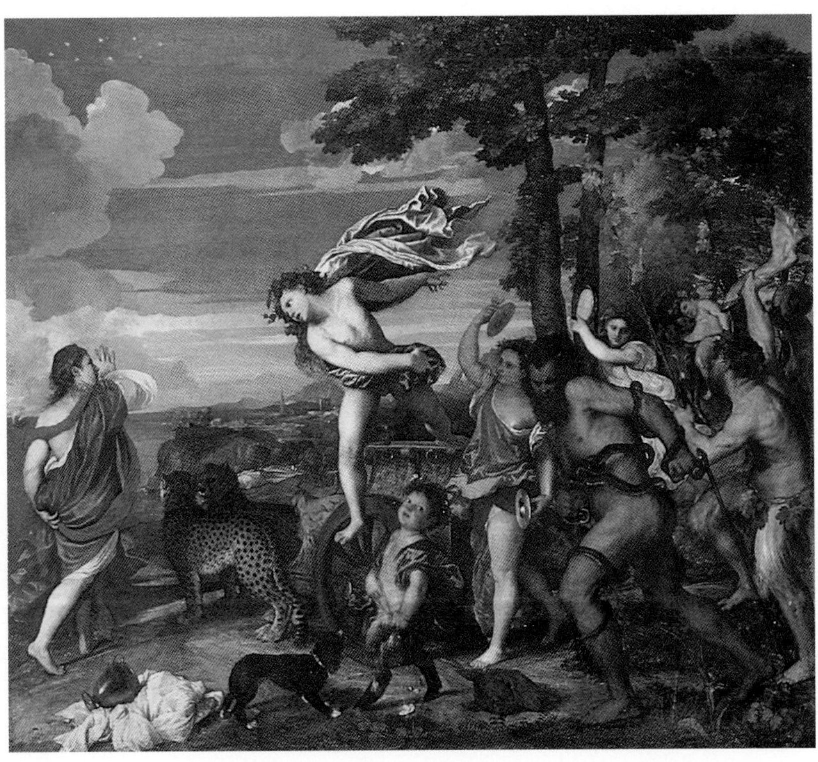

22. Titian: *Bacchus and Ariadne* (National Gallery, London)

does constitute something with which the painter can deliberately work, and make use of artistically. Indeed this is true of all works which are not *trompe l'oeil* pictures. A defining feature of *trompe l'oeil* is that when one is taken in by the depicted content one is not visually aware of the flat marked surface. The point I make here is that the awareness of the flat surface in conjunction with the depiction of space is a resource the painter can make use of. And of course it is not the case that all painters have been concerned with it.

A basic difference, then, between a tree and a picture of a tree, is that when we look at the picture we see a flat painted surface. And this allows the painter to present us with some visual effects which nature cannot put before us. The question arises of the artistic exploitation of these resources. Here are two examples of how this can be done.

In Pissarro's painting, the far side of the lane is seen both as running away from us into the picture plane, and as marking the lower side of a triangular wedge which sits on the picture plane. This effect accentuates something which can be found in nature: there is an evocation of it in Proust's *Remembrance of Things Past*. At a fashionable dinner party, the scholarly Brichot is holding forth on the etymology of place names:

> In any case, the river which gives its name to Dalbec is charming. Seen from one of the cliffs, it seems to lie just by the spires of the church, and almost seems to reflect them.
>   – I quite believe it, I said. It's an effect Elstir is very fond of. I've seen it in several sketches at his studio.[3]

In painting, however, the effect can be developed far beyond what is possible in nature. When we look at a real road we are presented with an edge which actually runs away from us into the distance. In the picture it is correct to see the line both as running into the picture plane *and* forming the lower side of a painted triangle.

A second example comes from the possibilities for the interaction of far and near as they are depicted in a painting. The example concerns the use of this device in the decoration of china tea cups, but of course it can be exploited in other places.

> Here is a young lady and courtly Mandarin, handing tea to a lady from a salver – two miles off. See how distance seems to set off respect. And here the same lady ... is stepping into a little fairy boat ... with a dainty mincing foot, which in a right angle of incidence (as angles go in our world) must infallibly land her in the midst of a flowery mead – a furlong off on the other side of the same strange stream.[4]

In this case, the juxtaposition of space and the flat surface on which space is depicted allow for special effects which nature cannot provide. The artistic exploitation of this resource differs from mere showmanship and makes the scene (a mandarin handing tea to a lady) richer in meaning and more poignant, more expressive of human relations, than a more naturalistic depiction of space.

In the middle years of this century it became something of an artistic *cause célèbre* to demand that a painting must be flat. This was derived from the perfectly correct observation that paintings are flat. It was then supposed to be some sort of lie for a painting to depict anything which was not flat, and thus to hide its true nature. But we can now see that condemnation to rest upon a simple confusion. Paintings, in general, do not engage with our spatial perception of the world by hiding their own flat surface, although that does occur in *trompe l'oeil* pictures. The decision to avoid the depiction of space can never be anything deeper than a stylistic choice. But it was not presented as a stylistic choice, it was presented as a moral necessity; to do otherwise was to play up to a lie, to embrace deception. Yet the claim that this flat style is more true to painting is a cultural superstition: we have seen that the depiction of space is quite compatible with visual awareness of the flat opaque surface.

6. Composition

Not all paintings exploit the sensuous qualities which derive from the traces of the application of paint. Various artists, and whole stylistic periods, have made a virtue of effacing these traces. This still leaves numerous ways in which one can be aware that the scene is painted. For example, the series of glazes and varnishes which painters apply to their work can be used to give the painting a silky surface texture which no grouping of objects could have in reality. Or, by omitting glazes, the painter can leave the work with a matte quality, which, again, no group of objects in reality could have.

One painting we have already looked at in which the traces of the brushstrokes have been meticulously covered over is Raphael's celebrated *Madonna of the Pinks* (plate 3). It is evident in this picture that the painter has devoted the greatest attention to the distribution of figures both in depicted space and in the outline they present on the surface plane of the canvas. There is also a subtle interaction between the two.

Raphael has not merely depicted the Madonna and Child; that is a function which many paintings accomplish. What he has also done is to resolve the lines and planes which depict the figures in an especially lucid way. It is this attention to the disposition of line and mass which gives the scene a super-worldly grace and dignity. In painting a complete control over contour and massing and resolution of these into harmonious ensembles can be achieved. And Raphael has exploited this special resource in the painting of this picture.

This resource, the resource of composition, and the great flexibility which painting allows for the composition to be resolved, the minute adjustments which can be made so that lines fall together gracefully, so that accents play off each other, so that complexity is contained within a simple overall design – this resource has here been employed for the creation of intrinsic value. But what exactly is it that is supposed to be intrinsically valuable in this case?

The picture has been described in terms of its content: Madonna and Child. It has also been noted how carefully the composition of the painting is handled. What this allows is an interaction between the two. Our vision of the Madonna-as-painted cannot be split into these two components. A remarkable integration of form and content has been achieved. I mention this last point only in passing; it is a point to which we shall return at greater length in the next chapter.

Looking at a painting is a dynamic process. The eye does not rest, stilled at a single point. Rather, it moves about the painting from one area of interest to another. One of the functions of composition is to encourage the eye to make certain transitions. In Canaletto's *Piazza San Marco dall'Ascensione* (plate 6) there is a framing device within the picture. We see the piazza through a depicted archway. Within the aperture of the archway, the campanile and the diagonal of the roof, depicted as running into the piazza, provide another frame for the roof-line of San Marco itself. Within this, a further frame is constructed leading the eye towards the centre of the painting. We see that the vertical edge of the campanile and the receding roof are deliberately chosen: the tower is seen almost straight on (parallel to the picture plane) and the side buildings at a particular angle.

Such over-determination of the point of view is perceived as intentional. As we stand looking at the picture, we recognise that the picture shows us the piazza from a very carefully chosen point of view; we are aware of the artist's sensibility in the selection of this point of view. This represents one of the most significant ways in which what is depicted (the piazza) differs from the depiction (the picture of the piazza). This is a possibility which emerges merely from the practice of depicting the world by means of paint.

The conclusion is that in being aware of these features one is necessarily aware of the way in which the subject matter, the piazza, has been 'formulated' not just 'in the medium' but within the potentialities of paint on a flat surface, and within the resources of depiction. Seeing the piazza 'framed' by an elaborate spatial composition is not to see a use of the medium as such. We see the formulation of the subject (the piazza) in the resources of the art-form.

7. Line

One of the predominant questions we are concerned with is how the experience of looking at a painted picture differs from the experience of looking at the things of which it is a picture. How does the experience of looking at a painting of a tree or of a square in Venice differ from looking at the tree or the square itself? The interest is not merely to catalogue the differences, but to think about how the experience of looking at the picture can be valuable in ways which are not available when we look at the real object.

We have, so far, seen three major ways in which the experiences may differ. First, we see the painted scene depicted in the medium of paint: our experience is shot through with an awareness that it is paint which is used to recreate something of the visual experience of looking at a piazza or a tree. Then we also see that the picture is a flat opaque surface: there is clearly no equivalent of this in ordinary perception of the world. We have seen, thirdly, how some pictures present their subject matter as viewed from a carefully chosen point of view. Each of these three ways gives the painter something to play with, something to exploit, in order to enrich the experience we have as we contemplate the picture: opportunities for the enrichment of experience which are not there when we stand looking at the real piazza or tree. We have seen how the painter can use the fact that it is paint which depicts the scene to introduce degrees of cohesion and to create accents of emphasis which do not exist among objects in the world, as when Cézanne paints rocks and fields with the same short, tense, architectural strokes.

When we look at a painted picture we have a sense of how what the artist does stands between us and the object depicted, and there are many factors which the painter can use in this field. In the Canaletto, it was the sense of point of view adopted. Other features which make us aware of the artist include the treatment of line and colour.

In some pictures, lines are conspicuously and skilfully arranged: either with an inherent grace as in Ingres or Perugino, or with a degree of distortion which could not exist in reality, or both. Examples of the latter occur in systematic elongation, when figures are given an unearthly lightness and slenderness, as seems to be the case with Perugino's angels. What happens here is that a naturalistic motif undergoes exaggeration. The motif is natural in that we do pay attention to outline when we look at objects in the world. Outline is something which the human perceptual system is naturally sensitive.

Sometimes line is emphasised as it can hardly be in reality. We are shown, perhaps, a bold contour or outline. One effect of this may be to bring the medium to our attention: we are made aware of the paint which is used to mark the outline. Apart from that, the painted contour emphasises a feature of the natural recognition of objects. For example, in Cézanne's still life studies, apples and pears are depicted with vigorous, thick outlines. Equally, line may be indistinct or suppressed in the picture in a way it never could be in reality, when in a picture an object is depicted without precise boundaries.

8. Symbolism and meaning

In Poussin's painting *A Roman Road* (plate 9), we are presented with a depiction of a road which has symbolic significance. As I walk down the street, I may, if I am in that sort of mood, think to myself, 'Life is rather like a road.' I look at the road and I have this thought. This is not what happens when we look at the painting. For in that case, we see a depiction of a road which is a symbol of life. Painted roads can be symbols, real roads can only be considered as, or treated as symbols: they are not symbols.

However, merely being a symbol is no great achievement. Symbols are inherently replaceable, for they are functional. Another symbol can have the same meaning. More particular to painting is the way in which the resources of depiction can be used to present the content in a uniquely affecting way.

For example, in Degas' portrait of Hélène Rouart (plate 7) the paint itself is a resource for conveying and enriching meaning. This is obvious enough when we notice the accuracy with which oil paint can render the significant movements of the eye and mouth which are so delicately linked to emotion. But the fact that the work is painted allows the painter control over features such as the relative proportion of the chair and the young woman: its largeness seems to squash her, or rather to show her as powerless; the chair emerges from the picture tilting towards us while Hélène Rouart herself remains behind. The control of the rendering of space gives the possibilities for a claustrophobic depiction. These depend upon the fact that in painting, as in all the graphic arts, the spatial relations have to be worked at by the artist in the successive actions of applying line and colour.

Further, the incompleteness of the painting of the chair, and the daub of blue which represents the woman's hand are potent sources of the elaboration of meaning. This is not a matter of illustration. The blue hand gives the painting of the woman a disturbing and expressive impact which can be achieved only through paint. Yet it seems almost like a human gesture, like an externalisation of human emotion. We smile when we are happy; if we felt like her, our hands might turn blue and disintegrate if they could. And to feel this, we need not be able to say exactly what that emotion is.[5] The painting stands as an example of how painting can acquire depth of meaning in virtue of being a painting. How the sitter has been painted lends a depth to her presentation, a depth which is irreducibly bound up in its articulation in paint; take paint away, and there is something we cannot articulate. This gives us some indication of what it is of value that painting can, uniquely, offer. Clearly there are experiences we have before this picture which we could not have when confronted with its sitter.

9. Conclusion: painting and photography

The list of resources described in this chapter is not, of course, complete. It serves, however, to show some of the opportunities that putting paint on canvas opens for the artist: opportunities to create objects which are of value to us. We have seen how that simple activity of applying pigment mixed in oil brings with it a range of possibilities which are poised for artistic exploration, and poised for the creation of intrinsically valuable objects. The sub-text is that other activities, such as flower arranging or baking bread or throwing stones in rivers, do not provide the creative artist with an equally extensive range of possibilities; they do not provide so many resources. This is a quantitative point. There is also a qualitative point: some of the resources, such as depiction, are of the highest order, for they give painting a direct link with perception at its most cognitively rich: looking at and responding to the visible world.

It is true that from almost anything, from old chairs, from broken flower pots, objects of interest can be made. But when we talk about the tremendous things in art, we are not talking about what is merely interesting, the attractive diversion of a moment, the passing smile of distraction. At its greatest painting can condense a vision of the world and the loves of a lifetime into an perpetual object which communicates these to others: when it is the great things which are at stake, then painting comes into its own.

The link with vision is something which painting shares with cinema, photography, theatre and sculpture. It has at times been said that photography has 'replaced' painting. The reasoning is that photography can more efficiently reproduce the two-dimensional appearance of objects. Suppose for the sake of argument that this is true, what of it? It tells us nothing about the ability of photography to replace painting. Because the value of a painting, as a work of art, never was confined to its ability to reproduce the two-dimensional appearance of an object. Depiction is one resource of painting and there is no reason to relinquish depictive painting because some other art-form also shares that resource. Yet this line has become one of the received ideas that plague conversation, forcing it into dead ends out of which one cannot turn.

Given the other resources which come into play, it is clear that a painted picture does not simply offer an image of the world. It offers an image which employs the varied resources of the art-form, and which invites the spectator to enjoy a certain perceptual experience. So a painted picture of the Thames, say, allows the image to be formed in the medium of paint, and in the resources of the art-form. And this cannot be replaced by anything else, for nothing but painting has those resources in which to formulate an image.

These visual resources serve the creation of intrinsic value: that is why they are relevant to the appreciation of paintings as works of art. And this has been the guiding thread of the present chapter. There are, obviously, many things which can be done with paintings which I have not mentioned (for example, they can be used in the decorative scheme of a room, a function not to be underestimated). I have tried to concentrate on ways in which painting can enable the creation of objects which are themselves valuable, without reference to anything beyond our visual experience when we contemplate them.

Visual experience must not be construed too narrowly. Satisfaction in vision involves, or at least can involve, the play of capacities which are not ordinarily or wholly visual. For example, our moral concerns come into play in visual experience: as when we see a charitable or a courageous act. As it stands this cannot immediately concern the appreciation of a painting as a work of art. Suppose I am pleased by the 'moral message' of Poussin's *Roman Road*. That moral concern, a concern with the role of endurance, endeavour and perseverance in life, cannot on its own lend the work artistic value; many another painting or description could convey the same message. Nevertheless, this moral concern is alive in the appreciation, and Poussin has exercised artistry in his handling of it. What we value is *this* moral rendered in paint in the precise *way* in which Poussin has rendered it.

In the next chapter we go on to look at some of the specific ways in which the resources so far discussed are used artistically in the creation of intrinsic value. It constitutes the heart of the book, for it is there that we see the most telling of connections: the connection between the opportunities uniquely present in painting and the achievements special to painting.[6]

Notes

1. Marcel Proust, *Remembrance of Things Past*, vol. 1, *Combray*, translated by C.K. Scott Moncrieff and Terence Kilmartin, Penguin, 1983, p. 195.

2. Dostoevsky, *The Idiot*, translated by Alan Myers, Oxford University Press, 1992, p. 64.

3. Marcel Proust, *Remembrance of Things Past*, vol. 5, *Sodome et Gomorrhe*, Gallimard Folio edition, p. 329. The translation is my own.

4. Charles Lamb, 'Old China' in *Elia and Last Essays of Elia*, Methuen, 1903, p. 248.

5. For the purposes of this example, it does not matter whether Degas intended the painting to be viewed as I have suggested. The discussion does not turn upon the precise meaning of this picture, but upon how paintings can have meaning.

6. This chapter presupposes a 'resemblance' account of depiction. That is, for p to depict o it is necessary (but not sufficient) that p resemble o. This view requires a careful elaboration of the kind of resemblance which holds between p and o. For analysis of the relevant kind of resemblance see M. Budd, *Values of Art*, London, 1995.

5

Achievements of Painting

1. 'By whom our eyes are opened'

I have just written a little study in the philosophy of art, if I may use that slightly pretentious phrase, in which I have tried to show how the great painters initiate us into acquaintance with and love of the external world, how they are the ones 'by whom our eyes are opened', opened, that is, on the world. In this study I take the work of Chardin as exemplary; I try to show his influence on our life, the charm and wisdom with which it layers our quotidian life and how it initiates us into the *life* of still life. Do you think this sort of study would interest the readers of the *Revue hebdomadaire*?

Letter from Marcel Proust to the editor of the
Revue hebdomadaire, November 1895[1]

'Well,' the question ought to come, 'what is it exactly that painters are supposed to open our eyes to?'

Notoriously, we are poor observers. We tend to see only what is expected, we are guided by habit. So it comes about often enough that we simply fail to notice the unexpected variation or the small change. This dependence on habit is true only for the most part. As with many an interesting generalisation, there are people who treat it as an inflexible truth: we only ever notice what we expect, what we have been indoctrinated to notice. If this were true we should be unable to cross the road without getting killed. We avoid getting killed because we have been schooled to be attentive, to look out for the unexpected. Sometimes at least our eyes have a fresh curiosity about the visible world, we search out detail and take pleasure in observation. In this respect painting can serve us well. Many a painter has been motivated by observation and a desire, even a need, to respond to and trace out that observation. It can hardly be surprising that this devotion often enough provides the less dedicated with guidance.

A sceptic might laugh here: 'But if you don't notice an effect when it is under your nose every day, how can you start noticing it when it is presented in a picture?' Painting has resources of isolation and accentuation. Take Chardin's *The Silver Goblet* (plate 10). This picture makes the reflections of the apples in the polished silverware particularly evident. By a careful use of compositional devices, Chardin makes the reflections catch our eye more easily than they normally would. The reflection in the goblet of the red of the apples is bordered on the left by a dull grey. This dull setting heightens the visual impact of the red: our eyes are drawn to the strongly marked contour where the two colour-patches meet. A second strategy Chardin employs is to make the reflected apples compositionally continuous with the apples themselves. The reflections in the goblet complete a crescent started by the three apples. If we follow this curve up to the right it terminates in the spoon handle. Thirdly, the greenish background makes the red-orange of the diffuse reflections in the bowl more apparent to the eye by means of contrast. There is even a touch of green on the side of the bowl facing us which brings this contrast even more to the fore. In these three ways the painter has made the reflected colours more apparent in the the picture than they would normally be, and this encourages us to dwell on them.

In such ways the painter can draw our attention to features of the visible world which we in our haste and habit tend to miss; the painter does this not simply by noticing and recording, but by employing the resources of the art-form to make such visible phenomena more apparent than they would otherwise be. All this holds equally of the great play the Impressionists made of the colours of shadows. Clearly, if they had simply represented this, we should be no more quick to notice them in the pictures than we are in the world. But what happens is that the colour of shadows is made into a theme in the pictures, so that the eye is drawn to them more than it would be in reality.

This kind of revelatory possibility has fostered a misunderstanding. Our century, inheriting an earlier obsession, has been in thrall to an image of the progress of science. Whatever our moral judgment on the final benefits of science, we cannot help but be astonished at the continued expansion of the scientific vision of reality and the precision and vastness of the command it can attain over the natural order. There clearly has been progress in scientific understanding. Whenever an image works well in one field there is an impulse to apply it elsewhere, sometimes with unfortunate results.

Thus people have long been keen to see such things as the colour of shadows as highly important in the history of art. And just as one likes to link the great scientist to his or her discoveries, there is a temptation to link great artists to a series of discoveries. And so, people seem almost hypnotised by the idea that, for example, Chardin is a great painter because he discovered the interplay of reflection, or that the Impressionists were important because they discovered the colour of shadows.

But this is quite misleading, for all its charm. For a start, it could simply have been pointed out by any observant person that the surfaces of neighbouring colours reflect each other. It does not take an artist to notice such things, and it does not take artistry to make them evident to others. Perhaps there are pamphlets by some Hampshire clergyman, writing well before Chardin, with titles such as *Notes on the Peculiar Co-reflection of Propinquous Coloured Surfaces* or *Studies in the Colour of Shadows*. These dusty papers, let us imagine, tell us exactly whatever it might be supposed Chardin or the Impressionists discovered. And if there are such papers they take nothing at all away from the artistic greatness of those painters. For it was not merely noticing these phenomena which was important. It was the ability to make these observations tell artistically, to find in them the material out of which a work of art could be made. For all his acuity, the supposed Hampshire clergyman never set out to do that. It is not discovery but use which counts when it comes to the art of painting.

It can hardly be doubted that there are many natural phenomena of real beauty to which our attention has been drawn by painters. And at least some of them would remain unnoticed had they not been seen and depicted by painters. Thus, to speak personally, I had never noticed how delightful a grey cloud can be against a pure blue sky. I had somehow always assumed that there would be a white cloud in between. The phenomenon was brought to *my* notice by Poussin, and I am grateful to him for that.

But for all that, it is not convincing to link this sort of awakening to the excellence of the painter. It is undoubtedly the case that our sensitivity to these phenomena is fostered by derivative and second-rate painters just as much as it is by the innovative and the fine. One might first come to see the grey and blue together under the guidance of an otherwise very poor work, or without the guidance of any painting whatever. Actual influence is too much hostage to fortune to be a proper measure of artistic greatness.

So we discover a second way in which something to which painters can open our eyes – certain effects of natural beauty – does not simply correlate with artistic excellence.

The revelation which Proust has in mind in the essay mentioned at the start of this chapter is rather different. In this essay (which, incidentally, was not taken up by the editor of the review) he asks us to consider a young man disaffected with the circumstances of his unexceptional life and the ordinariness of the objects by which he is surrounded. He consoles himself in imagination with dreams of wealth and of a life in which he is surrounded by art and luxury down to the door handles, a fantasy reminiscent of Flaubert's longed-for 'Wonderful Winter' – to be passed in Paris serenaded by hummingbirds and eating off plate designed for a Borgia Pope – it would, Flaubert adds realistically, certainly not cost more than twelve billion francs for the season.

When this young man escapes from the family dining-room to the Louvre, Proust guides him to the Chardin room, where are gathered the small, carefully observed still-lifes and domestic scenes for which that artist is famous. There is one picture which particularly attracts the young man's attention. He is delighted by *Saying Grace* (plate 12). Proust's point is that Chardin himself looked upon a scene such as the young man has just disdained at home. The difference is that Chardin was able to find in such a scene the inspiration for a painting.

It is not that Chardin simply larded dreary objects with affection; he found a beauty and a charm in them. It is not that Chardin noticed detail which is otherwise difficult to spot. Rather he has uncovered a general quality of the scene, a general quality which does not fully reside in any particular detail. To take a parallel, imagine you notice that someone has acted with tact. It is not a single detail, their tactfulness, which you have noticed. In seeing certain things they do not do, and certain things they do and say, moments when they are silent, or when they put someone at ease, you notice across the whole that they are acting tactfully. Detail comes to be emotionally alive in the ensemble, precisely through its connection to other things. The fact that these other things are not all material, for we are referring sometimes to intention, or to what is not done, to reserve and virtues of omission, does not prevent this from being a visual perception.

It is to such diffuse qualities, which are not fully grasped in any particular detail but which speak through many details together, that Proust appeals in describing the picture:

> Friendship exists, wedlock even ... between the stooping body, the happy hands, of the woman who is laying the table and the old table-cloth with still unchipped plates, whose gentle tenacity she has felt for so many years always holding its own in her careful grasp, between the table-cloth and the sunlight which as a keepsake of their daily encounters has given it the smoothness of cream or of a linen lawn, between the sunlight and the whole of this room that it fondles, where it falls asleep, where now it loiters, now frisks into when least expected – exists with all the tenderness of years between warmth and materials, between beings and things, between past and present, between light and shade.[2]

There is a kind of depression in which the world is felt to be empty of value. And this can be of a piece with how the world looks. This is not a matter of detail: the sunlight still strikes the tree at the same point, the leaves are of the same colour and tone, the puddles reflect as they always have done. Only we are dead to it. What happens then when perception comes alive and is animated by enjoyment, by love? Two things at least, and they are the subject of the next two sections of this chapter. Our sense of detail is absorbed into a greater appetite of perception: a vision of the picture or the scene as a whole. Secondly, we experience the full range of our powers coming together in the play of perception.

So, the revelatory power of painting is not so much that it can show us beauties to which we might otherwise be blind (although it can do this) and lead us to satisfaction where it would otherwise be unexpected. Gratitude is owed for this, but this point does not really get us very far with what painting is able to do. If this 'discovery' were the correct account of our interest in painting, then our interest would be exhausted the moment we assimilated the discovery. But that is not how our interest in painting works. We do not stop being interested in Chardin the moment we have learned to attend to subtle effects of light and colour for ourselves.

If revelation is important to appreciation, it will have to be more than this. What the picture reveals, what painting at the high reaches of artistry and imagination reveals, is what perception can be; it reveals a high point in the ways our eyes can find beauty and significance, the way all our capacities come together in an act of perception. And because this does raise us out of our usual condition it is something we experience as a revelation. It does not so much reveal an empirical fact about the observable world: it yields a quality of experience. As in a marriage one can be surprised again and again by the consoling persistence of love and repose, just as one can be surprised by the haunting return of pain. We are made to forget these things, recovering them is always fresh.

We turn, now, to a closer discussion of these two features of perception: the experiences of 'seeing together' and the 'unification of the self' which painting can yield.

2. Synthetic seeing

Depiction can serve our visual experience, and be found intrinsically valuable through the special opportunities it affords for *synthetic seeing*. This kind of seeing can be illustrated by a quotation from Proust. Here he is describing the experience of looking at a face, that of the literary predecessor of Madame de Guermantes.

> It is a face we have created from a certain look, from the line of her nose, a part of her cheek, one of the thousands of people we make emerge from a single person. Presently another face will constitute that person for us. Soon she is her pale skin and her shoulders which seem to trace a disdainful shrug. Now she is the sweet, almost timid, shape of her face in which the opposition of her white cheeks and black hair no longer plays a part.[3]

Proust's virtue as a diviner of beauty is not that he can notice when others cannot that her cheek is thus and so or that her face is a certain colour. Rather, it is a matter of how he composes with elements which more or less anyone can see; he selects and runs together a movement of the eye, a part of a cheek, and the line of a nose, a nose from which mass and colouring have been excluded. This is an imaginative exercise *par excellence*: it is an exercise which is irreducibly visual, unlike the function of pointing out that shadows are, after all, coloured: something which can be as well said as shown.

The image of construction, synthesis or composition in seeing sheds light on something of which Chardin is a master. In order to see what is at stake in painting and the special way this can be achieved, let me turn back to the Corot picture which has so occupied our attention already. It is itself a comment that one can derive so much from looking at a single work.

Avignon from the West (plate 1) shows a particularly

wide expanse of foreground and yet Corot has managed to give the picture a compelling unity. This has much to do with the composition and at this stage I shall draw attention to just one point. Across the lower section of the canvas there runs a theme of triangles: the blue of the Rhône, the white building (on the left), the dark trees and lighter patch (on the right). This theme draws on the resources of the art-form. The similarity in the way in which the river, trees, farm and road have been rendered in paint strengthens the cohesion which we can see in the painted scene; strengthens it, that is, in comparison with the ways we could see those elements together if we stood on the spot (in space and time) Corot occupied when he painted his picture. The eye is brought to compose, in the contemplation of the painting, with a sureness and cohesion which goes beyond that afforded by the corresponding bit of reality.

In Chardin's picture *The Smoker's Case* (plate 11) we can hold together the goblets on the right and the left with a special degree of cohesion because they have been painted in a similar way, with a dense flattened texture which is still visibly pigment: this sets up a unity between the two sides of the canvas, a unity which depends upon the manner of depiction, thus going beyond the kind of unity we would be able to see among such items were we lucky enough to come across them so grouped in reality. Other themes are the use of blue, particularly the way in which it is taken up in the silver goblet and, more subtly, the simplification of colour and surface which is consistent across the whole picture. So, in this work, the painter elicits from the attentive spectator an intense experience of synthetic seeing. The spectator is induced into viewing the ensemble of objects as a whole and into the gradual assimilation of the layers of unification which the painter has imposed upon the depicted objects. This unification is developed in the handling of of paint, the composition, the selection of point of view, the softening of contours, harmonising of shapes and tones – that is, in the skilful exploitation of the resources of the art-form.

3. Seeing with

If we look at Poussin's *Self Portrait* in red chalk (plate 14) we see a face depicted as seen in a particular way, a way which we might try to describe with reference to a lack of forgiveness, harshness of judgment, remorse, self-questioning. The face is depicted as seen with feeling. How has Poussin achieved this? In this picture, various features of the depicted face and of the manner of the use of the medium leap to our attention: the turn of the mouth, the heavy lining of the cheeks, the emphasis of the features of the face over the loosely marked jacket. It is important, if the notion of depiction-as-seen-with is to stick, to distinguish this from the drawn observation of feeling. When Raphael draws a surprised face, as in the *Studies for Two Apostles* (plate 15) we are not tempted to call it a face depicted as seen with surprise: rather, it is the cool observation of a face which betrays emotion. This sharpens our question: can we say what it is about the Poussin drawing that makes us want to distinguish it from the Raphael drawing and say that the Poussin drawing depicts a face as seen with feeling and does not merely depict a face which shows emotion although it does of course, *inter alia*, depict a face which shows emotion?

We see the way the medium is used as expressive of the attitude or feeling of the maker; expressive, that is, of his attitude towards the object depicted. This is only one way we can see the lines. The appropriateness of seeing the lines this way does not rest upon it having been the case that the draughtsman did have that attitude. More relevant is the way he intended the lines to be seen. Intending a sequence of lines to be seen as expressive of rage or

despair is not in any way dependent upon feeling rage or
despair. Life, however, being what it is, we do prize
sincerity, but that cannot impinge upon what makes it
right to see a line as expressive. In the Poussin drawing,
the marking of the face with the red chalk, the emphasis
of certain areas of shadow, and the concentration of contour in the face so that the area bounded by the eyes and
mouth seems like a precipitate of the whole of the drawing,
provokes an impression of intensity. This impression depends upon the *way* the face has been drawn, with the
working of the surface becoming less dense as we move
away towards the edges of the paper.[4] Whereas when
looking at the Raphael drawing we see the contours used
in pursuit of a modelling of a face with the expressive force
the face has. Poussin has made use of the resources of
drawing to convey an attitude he has towards himself. He
depicts himself *as seen with* a heightened feeling of disgust.

Depiction works by the exploitation of the resources of
a medium to produce an image which – in respect of
two-dimensional features – looks like the object of which
it is a picture. Such exploitation brings with it opportunities for control of the look of the depicted object which have
no counterpart in the formation of patterns of perception
independent of depiction. A depicted face can be isolated,
or presented monochromatically, or can dissolve and so
on, in ways in which no real face could be monochromatic,
isolated or made to dissolve. This point applies too when
we consider what connections there might be between the
look of a face when seen with self-loathing and the depiction of a face as seen with self-loathing. The resources of
the art-form present the skilful artist with opportunities
for the heightening, simplifying, exaggeration, selection,
suppression, and so on, of the features which were relevant to the look of the face when seen with feeling

self-loathing. This may be brought out more clearly with reference to the Poussin drawing.

The monochrome treatment of the drawing adds to the sense of how the feelings which dominate around the centre of the face spread out across the whole of the drawing. In this way the continuity between areas of shadow is greater in the picture than it would have been when Poussin looked at himself. The shadow to the right of the nose is close in tone to the shadow between collar and neck; on the left, the marks are made to run more or less parallel to each other. The scoring of that same cheek seems to run down into the lapel of the jacket: a continuity achieved in the drawing. The very sketchiness of the jacket, as already remarked upon, seems to give the expression of the face a terrible predominance. The lines of the cheeks run up towards the eyes, carrying the disgust of the mouth up to the searching eyes.

4. Transience

Paintings can make vivid to us aspects of perceptual experience which normally elude our attention. One such aspect of experience is the fleeting quality of time and of the satisfactions which exist in time.

The Rokeby Venus (plate 13) by Velásquez has been interpreted as representing the transitoriness of youth. If this is correct, then the picture represents something which it does not depict. Ordinarily, to see the fleeting quality of youthful loveliness one would have to watch a suitable person over a period of time, as she changed. But this picture does not depict the young woman across time, it depicts her at a particular moment in time. The transition from youth to age is something which can be observed, but the picture does not present us with such an extended observation. If this picture does represent the fleetingness of youth it does so by means other than depicting it.

Someone who can observe the passage of youthful bloom in another is not, thereby, sufficiently equipped to grasp that this picture represents the fleetingness of youth. This content is not naturally generated by the spectator. Obviously, too, this picture does not show us a scene which looks like the fading of youthful bloom. This content, the transience of youth, fails two tests of ordinary depiction.

Nevertheless, Velásquez has rendered this non-depicted content palpable and vivid; our sense of the transitoriness of youth is liable to be more excited when contemplating this picture than it is when looking at some real person whose bloom is, albeit slowly, fading. There are many details of the way in which this work has been created which act in consort to achieve such a strong effect.

Velásquez has devoted great attention to linear composition: the woman's body is presented in a series of curves which open one into the other, without any sense of closure. This is particularly evident around her upper hip; the line which delineates the hip flows into her lower back and there disappears, while another line marking her ribs begins, only to fade out somewhere in her shoulder. The line which depicts the contour of her left buttock fades into the small of her back.

Compositionally, her body, though very elegant, is restless. The extended right arm, in particular, presents a fluid abstract shape on the surface of the canvas, and this is true also of the depiction of the legs. We are encouraged to notice the shapes of the marked surface by the disposition of colour. The body area is set out very clearly from the dark sheet on which the woman reclines. The long curving folds of the sheets of the divan have, by contrast, a tonic completeness. The multitude of minor contours is taken up in a single and simple dominant curve flowing from one side of the canvas to the other. The Cupid and Venus are compositionally balanced, but only in a precarious way. Her right arm and his wing form 'rhyming' structural entities. If we take the swag of the curtain as an axis, then the whole compact mass of Cupid (although his limbs look as if they have been squeezed out of a tube) forms a balancing weight to the torso of Venus, from buttocks to shoulders. This is the key relation of mass in the picture. A line running along the top of his wing and arms curves gently into the shoulder and upper arm of Venus, producing a degree of continuity, but one which is more suggested than asserted. The instability of this major structural pairing is intensified by the fluid space between the legs of each figure. This is the fulcrum between the two major masses of the picture, and rather than it being a point of strength, it is an area of looseness and movement.

Between these precariously balanced figures are placed the highly distinctive straight edges and precise angles of the mirror and its frame; although even here the recursive loops of ribbon sound again the notes of the two bodies. And within the frame the image of a lovely face shimmers, in contrast to the sharp definition of the frame.

What I have enumerated above are elements which serve to produce a very strenuous composition, which nevertheless as a total has a high degree of repose. The image of the lovely face lies at the intersection of many lines of tension within the work. Because of this, many parts of the work which are physically disparate are linked compositionally to the face. The elements I have picked out are dynamic ones which have, through the brilliant arrangement of the artist, achieved a stasis: the tensions hold one another in check, yet they all remain. I am not claiming that this is an analogue for the bloom of youth. Rather, the point is that we experience a degree of concentration of disparate elements held together with a momentary ease. Thus the composition serves to fix attention on the face within a very fluid composition.

The painter signals the interpretation of the passing of

beauty in a special way. The mirror and the ribbons are taken from the familiar theme of the *Vanitas* picture, which takes its name from the well-known passage in Ecclesiastes: 'Vanity, all is vanity!' Traditionally, mirrors and ribbons were among the objects used by painters as symbols of the insubstantiality of earthly pleasures. Velásquez could count on his spectators to be well acquainted with these symbols, which are, in any case, not entirely arbitrary.

Thus the spectator is prompted to see the picture with this thought in mind. And with this thought in mind the passing bloom is made vividly present to us. We can see, then, that to appreciate this painting the spectator must know something about the symbolic meaning of mirrors and ribbons within the tradition of painting. If the vividness of the passing of beauty is dependent upon seeing the picture with this point in mind, then we have further explanation of why the transience of youthful beauty is not properly speaking depicted in this picture. Recognition of this content relies upon knowledge of symbolic conventions, and this is knowledge which is not required just to see pictures as pictures or to see youthful beauty passing in reality.

However, it would be quite mistaken to derive from this dependence upon stipulated symbolism that the picture merely represents the idea of the passage of youthful beauty. For to represent that idea is not thereby to produce the phenomenological impact which this work achieves. Schiller's stanza:

> By the stream sat a youth,
> Weaving flowers into a wreath;
> He saw them carried off
> And swept along in the dancing waves.
> 'Thus my days speed by
> Relentlessly, like the stream!
> And my youth grows pale,
> As quickly as the wreaths wilt!'[5]

communicates the idea of the fleeting quality of youth, but it does not give us a vivid visual impression of seeing youth fade. If Velásquez's picture worked merely by exploiting conventional symbols it could not produce the visual impression it does, although, like Schiller's poem, it could effectively communicate the idea of transitoriness. When we seek to *explain* the way in which Velásquez has made vivid the fleeting quality of youthful beauty, we cannot merely point to the symbolism he exploits. That symbolism is quite inadequate to explain the visual impression the work makes.

5. Transcendence

There are many concepts which articulate things of great importance in our experience: concepts like 'death', 'love', 'hope', 'vice'; but no instance of these concepts, no particular death, no particular gesture of love, no particular vice or occasion of hope, actually makes the full significance of these concepts present to us. The meaning of such great ideas transcends anything which ordinary experience can instantiate. Their full grandeur cannot be encompassed within single instances.

The representation of one very special concept, that of God, has particularly exercised painters. The representation of God presents the problems already mentioned in an acute form. The concept 'God' has no visual determinants, that is, there is no proper description of what God looks like. In his *Guide for the Perplexed*, Maimonides elaborates the classic argument against the depiction of God: God is abstract and so representation is always false, and to pursue the false (or a false) presentation of God is a form of idolatry: any visual representation of God is a betrayal, because a visual image necessarily conveys an erroneous picture of God. Whenever one makes an image of God it cannot be God one has made a picture of because God is beyond any visual image.

At the same time, because this concept brings together so many concerns about the origins and purpose of the world and about the meaning of life, giving ourselves a vivid visual representation of this concept which makes its significance palpable will be a valuable cultural achievement. And, of course, one does not have to be personally exercised about the concept 'God' to see that this type of problem occurs widely: the attempt to make visually vivid some concept whose full significance is not revealed in its visible manifestations, if indeed it has any. I discuss the concept 'God' simply as a striking instance of a general issue.[6]

In *Elijah with the Angel* (plate 16) by Gaspard Dughet, God is represented by the small figure of an old, bearded man emerging from the clouds. Merely to represent God in this way would not be to provide a vivid image of divinity and divine power. There are various means, however, which Dughet has exploited to give us a visual impression of divine power. But all this depends upon the fact that we already know, from the title and general cultural understanding, that this depicted figure represents God the Father. With this assumption in place, however, the painter can go on to generate a vivid image, in which the force of the image does not depend merely upon culturally learned associations.

One strategy Dughet employs is to make the depiction of the bearded man resonate across the wider spaces of the canvas. The dark cloud from which the figure emerges has been painted with parallel slanting brushstrokes. These brushstrokes are exactly at a right angle to the main axis of the figure and they are parallel with the second most important axis of the figure. The dark grey of the old man's beard and hair merge into the cloud so that one cannot say exactly where his hair ends and where the cloud begins.

Thus the man seems to be continuous with the cloud, or the cloud with him. It is as if the power of the cloud and its threatening aspect has become concentrated at this point where it takes on the shape of a man; it is also as if the man extends as largely and impressively as the cloud.

If we concentrate for a moment on the surface pattern, we see that the three most prominent branches converge, from three corners of the canvas, upon a single area, and it is in the middle of this area that the figure of God is located. This area is further emphasised by the dark line of cloud above and the dark mountain ridge below, a pair of curves which mirror each other and which focus on the figure in the clouds. The painter's artistry is impressive, for not only do these devices succeed in making the little figure prominent in the work, they do so in a way which is not too obvious: the branches look naturalistic, the line of the cloud and the ridge of mountains seem at first sight to be placed in an uncalculating way. The figure of God the Father also lies at the apex of some important triangular forms in the picture. The blue mountains in the far distance, on the left, and the nearer slopes on the right, would – if continued – meet close to the point where the figure emerges from the clouds.

It is important to note that these relations exist on the surface of the canvas, not in the represented three-dimensional space. The male figure is not depicted as lying between the branches; he is much further away than the trees. Rather, the area of canvas on which the figure is depicted lies between the areas on which the branches are depicted. And the same holds for the relation of the figure to the slopes of the mountains. The carefully muted architecture of the work allows the prominence of the figure in the clouds to be slightly mysterious: our eye is continuously drawn to it, but it is not obvious – at first – why this is so; the figure has a visual magnetism out of proportion to its size or colouring. We have now seen something of the elaborate means by which Dughet achieves this.

The figure of God is linked with the cloud and is carefully placed within the surface arrangement of the work. On this basis Dughet is able to follow through further effects which give a visual image of God's power. The dark cloud becomes darker towards the top left of the picture and is depicted as extending beyond the bounds of the picture: the limits of the cloud are not depicted. This does not, on its own, suggest that what is depicted is limitless; but as we already know that the picture represents God, unbounded representation of the cloud gives a visual equivalent of the unbounded power of God. At the same time, the lower part of the picture shows a dramatic opposition of light and dark: the shadow cast by the cloud is depicted falling over the land. The effects of the storm on the trees are evident, but the agitation of the picture extends beyond this: the broken tree on the lower right and the violently twisting form of the path are continuous with the agitation of the storm even though they are not effects of the storm.

In quite specific ways we can describe how the painter manages to present an image which makes the power of God visually vivid. This achievement depends, to a certain extent, upon the assumption that the spectator knows that the figure in the cloud represents God. Armed with this knowledge, however, the spectator is presented with a scene painted in such a way as to make that figure visually very important and to concentrate the depiction of power in that figure, so that the power of the storm becomes the power of that figure. In doing this, the painter has exploited resources which are particular to painting, especially the manner of controlling the brushstrokes and the two-dimensional arrangement of shapes (although they depict three-dimensional objects).

6. Conclusion

This chapter has considered ways in which paintings can have special content. This content is dependent upon the way in which these pictures have been painted: it concerns what the resources of painting can be exploited to show us. Yet it has been emphasised already in earlier chapters that content on its own cannot generate artistic value. The artistic value depends upon precisely how the content has been formed in a particular painting: not just what has been depicted but how.

This chapter has concentrated on the grand content of some artistically successful works; grand content, however, can be the downfall of a work of art. Suppose a work takes on a major theme, but the painter has nothing substantial to communicate on that theme, worse, he has some confused, clichéd and sentimental notions about it. This explains why it is often so misleading to discuss a work simply in terms of 'what it is about' – a favourite technique of critics. It is the easiest thing in the world to paint a picture which is 'about the relation between generations and the sexes': any stick-drawing of a family would suffice for that. The difficulty is to have something significant to communicate about the subject matter.

Another difficulty is to provide an image which makes the content visually vivid. I do not think that Dughet has anything special to communicate about God in the picture discussed above, nor is it clear that Velásquez had elaborate theses about time which he was trying to communicate. What these painters have done, however, is to provide a compelling visual image in which we seem to see some important idea, an idea which is usually not visibly present to us.

Notes

1. Marcel Proust, 'Essais et Articles', edited by Pierre Clarac and Yves Sandre, to be found appended to the Pléiade Edition of *Contre Sainte-Beuve*, Gallimard, 1971. My translation.

2. Marcel Proust, 'Portraits of Painters: Chardin' in *By Way of Sainte Beuve*, translated by Sylvia Townsend Warner, Chatto and Windus, 1958. The essay on Chardin was never finished.

3. My translation.

4. It is very important to recognise that even in this case there is clearly a good deal of 'cool' or detached consideration at work on the part of Poussin, in disposing his expressive marks upon the paper so that a poised, highly controlled image emerges.

5. From 'The Youth by the Brook' translated by Richard Wigmore in *Schubert: The Complete Song Texts*, Victor Gollancz, 1988.

6. This problem has a distinguished intellectual history. The most prominent discussion is Kant's in *The Critique of Judgment*, section 49.

6

Style and Expression

1. Concepts of style

'Style' and 'expression' are complex notions used to describe *how* depicted content is rendered. Broadly similar depicted content can be painted in different styles and with different expressive qualities. The development and elaboration of styles and the mastery of expressive force are central achievements of painting practised as an art.

Neither term, however, is a lucid one. What exactly is it that we appreciate when we admire the style or expression of a work? Answering this involves saying what we mean by 'style' or 'expression'. Different writers have used the terms in different ways. In what follows I try to pick out central concerns which these terms have been used to signal. It is those concerns, obviously, and not the words themselves which are of importance.

'Style' can be understood in at least two different ways. There is the general use of stylistic terms, for example 'Rococo style', which can apply equally to many artists. A second way in which the term is used is of an individual painter. Thus we can talk about Titian's style, or Corot's style; although this style can change or develop or degenerate it is unique to an individual. These two uses of the term have some important features in common. This common ground can be illustrated by considering a case from outside the arts.

Copperplate is a style of script. There are numerous distinctive features copperplate has which differentiate it from other styles of writing. It provides a guide as to how letters are to be formed, the prevailing slope of the script, the rhythm of thicker and thinner strokes, the relation of loops to straight lines, and so on. Having any one of these features (e.g. slope) does not entail having any of the others (e.g. the way the letter *p* is formed). The *style* brings together the whole set of devices and practices which do not have to go together.

It brings them together, as a style, because of the effect of 'going together' which they are discovered to have. And also for the sake of certain aesthetic effects which, together, they promote: neatness, gracefulness, clarity and a strong sense of rhythm.

Putting these two points together, we have a rudimentary notion of style. A style brings together a set of guidelines, techniques and practices which govern all aspects of how the script will look. And this is done for the sake of certain characteristic aesthetic effects.

This model can be applied to both individual style and general style in painting. In each case, a style of painting is understood as a set of practices and devices which are experienced as having a high degree of consistency – they are found to go well together – which governs how the picture is to be made. And these exist for the sake of particular aesthetic effects.

A style is personal or general depending upon the way in which it is formed. When a particular painter in his own work gradually pieces together a complete and coherent set of techniques and guides which suit his own aesthetic purposes, then we say that he has developed a personal style. Others who are influenced by his work can take up this set of techniques. In so doing, they are adopting a general style: something they did not discover for themselves and which others too may adopt.

Personal style *could* develop as a means of expression of personality: a painter might gradually develop a mode of painting until it is the perfect vehicle for the expression of his personality. But I think that this is forced as a general description of individual style in painting, although it might work in literature. From their contrastive individual styles of painting we sense a difference in character between Michelangelo and Leonardo. But it would be rash, on the basis of pictures alone, to make detailed claims about the character of each painter as a man. When personality is expressed, however, we would expect to learn something about personality. This suggests that personal style of painting does not really convey very much *about* the personality of the painter. Even though individual style is closely tied to the development of an individual painter, it does not follow that the style will be a mirror of the man.

Working with this notion of style, we can ask whether full appreciation of a painting as a work of art requires a grasp of the style of the work. Take Koch's engravings from around 1800 which illustrate the story of Jason. I shall consider the tableau in which Jason is depicted presenting Orpheus to the Argonauts (plate 18). This engraving is heavily indebted to the style of figure drawing developed in the decoration of Greek vases. Thus the emphasis of line and of profile, the proportion of limbs, the posture of depicted figures, the fall of drapery (and so on) are garnered from the vases. When one sees these features of the work one might think that Koch had himself adumbrated these integrations, that it was Koch who by a great feat of imagination found that an emphatic linearity works extremely well with a predominant nudity and with certain postures and with an understated facial expression. But these integrations are not Koch's work. The idea of integrating these features is one adopted by him.

There are at least two ways in which grasping that the

work is in a particular style is relevant to full appreciation of it as a work of art.

Some of the properties which the line is intended to be seen as having depend upon its being in a style. Relative to a given style, the depiction of particular forms can be correct or incorrect. In the Greek style, there are conventions governing proportions of depicted limbs. In his depiction, Koch adheres to these conventions. The proportions of Jason's limbs are correct relative to the style in which Koch is working. Clearly, a depiction can be correct in this sense without being accurate. Merely being correct, in this way, cannot furnish an appropriate reason for valuing the picture as a work of art. For many pictures instantiate these correct proportions, so mere correctness does not give us ground to value any one of them as irreplaceable (which is a necessary condition for valuing it as a work of art).

However, this does not mean that correctness cannot figure in an appropriate reason (in support of a judgment of artistic value). Koch, for example, has integrated correctness of proportion with the other properties of the picture: its clear narrative, its massing of figures, its expressive qualities. He has also given them a particular set of correct proportions (there is in principle more than one way of doing this). Thus, there are particular qualities (unique to this picture) the description of which involves reference to correct proportion. This means that correct proportion can figure in appropriate reasons for evaluation of artistic merit.

Further, understanding the history of the style, we savour the appropriateness of using a Greek style of figuration to illustrate a Greek story. This depends upon grasping not only the style of the engraving, but also its provenance. So there is content which we can only recognise if we wield a notion of style such as has been outlined so far. Without this notion we could not see the appropriateness of illustrating this story in this way.

A peculiarity of the engraving is the landscape setting which has no precedent on Greek vases. The landscape is depicted in quite a different manner, indeed in a contemporary (early nineteenth-century) style, from the figures which inhabit it. The aesthetic effect produced by the landscape is quite different from that of the figures. The landscape is extravagantly varied with cliffs, pools and wooded hills. Part of understanding the picture requires that we realise that these two manners of depiction do not usually go together, on top of grasping the fact that the work brings together these two manners of depiction.

But how can this matter for the appreciation of the engraving as a work of art? The spectator is invited to take pleasure in the integration of two manners of depiction, but not only that. We are invited to enjoy this particular integration of *this* depiction of figures (in the Greek style) and *this* depiction of the landscape (in a contemporary style); this integration is part of the meaning of the picture, and we cannot see it without seeing this etching. In this respect (providing this particular integration of these two manners) the etching is irreplaceable. For even though there are several works in the series which integrate these two styles, in each case it is done in a slightly different way. So there is a specific description, which none the less refers ineliminably to the integration of styles, which holds for each of these etchings.

In each of these cases, the notion of style, as formulated, is indispensable for the full appreciation of these works.[1]

2. Concepts of expression

When I look at Daubigny's 1872 picture, *Alders* (plate 19), one of the things that holds my attention is the depicted reflection of the colours of the sky, broken and juxtaposed with local colours, playing on the water. In looking at the depicted reflection, I am drawn towards employing vocabulary derived from the emotions. Thus I wish to refer to the quietness and tranquillity of the depicted scene, and to something private and sombre about it, a sense of isolation and of being alone, of a specific quality of time: it is a very particular moment of the day which is depicted. But this sense of particularity of the spot is set off against the implicit, slightly veiled, immensity and glowing sublimity of the sky. The sky – for all its vastness – is recalled in the reflections of the water: all that immensity is contained now within the small body of water, there among the pond-weed and the ducks. A number of features of the depicted trees join in with these responses: the silhouette, the lush, dank greens of the lower portions; the most bloated green is just at the margin (barely visible in the reproduction) and one can hardly tell whether it depicts land or water; the heavy sense of shade. All these features set off and contrast with the alders bearing their lighter leaves high into the evening light, catching something of its dying glow, and with the slender, at times ungainly, trunks tracing their lines of shadow over the brightest portion of the sky. The cool colouring of the left of the canvas – the greater expanse of pale blue in the sky, the blue of the far hills, the darker shadows of the trees – presents the visual chill of the approach of night, and this chill is beginning to move across the surface of the water from left to right. This coolness contrasts with a warmth which lingers to the right in the depiction in the sky and particularly in the reflected pinks and oranges.

This picture is observant of certain visual effects of evening, and so far I have spoken largely in terms of content, but what I am responding to is the content as depicted, as painted: the colours of the water, the spread of the sky as realised within the resources of the art-form; the smudged effect of more distant foliage; the short dabs with which the pond-weed is depicted; the delicate way in which the ducks are differentiated from the weed with just a tiny curve of the brush; the play of horizontal and vertical lines with which the water is represented.

This is an expressive picture. The term 'expression' is often used loosely, and we can ask what exactly is being attributed to this work, or what different things might be attributed to it, in calling it expressive.

A first thought is that one is claiming that the artist felt an emotion when he painted it, and that the work stands as an *expression* or externalisation of the artist's feeling, like an immensely sophisticated gesture. This may have been the case, but it is not what I am concerned about. It is quite possible for a painting to be expressive in *this* (gestural) sense and give no spectator the sense of its being expressive. In fact, Daubigny painted several pictures rather like this one, all of which are (more or less) similarly expressive. It seems to me highly improbable that there was a single feeling which he was continuously trying to express.

Alternatively, we might think that the picture causes a feeling in the spectator, and this is what makes the picture expressive of that feeling. But this cannot be quite right. The work is expressive of melancholy, but it does not make me feel melancholy. It affects me, but not by instilling in me the feeling of which it is expressive.

'All right,' someone might say, 'its being expressive is neither to do with being caused by the artist's feeling, nor to do with causing that feeling in the spectator. Let's say then that the picture just *stands for* the feeling: it's a sort of complex sign. It's a bit like someone *saying*: "I don't know why I feel so sad when I look at the trees at dusk".' But this rather bloodless notion, that the picture communicates the idea of being sad, cannot be the whole truth. For the impact that the picture is liable to make upon the spectator is not merely a communication about the notion of sadness: sometimes people feel sad at sunset, especially when they are contemplating nature. The picture makes this feeling vivid to us, but not by causing us to feel melancholy ourselves.

The notion of expression which we are looking for must be this: the picture makes vivid to the spectator something of *what it is like* to feel melancholy at sunset. And one can grasp this (and enjoy it) without feeling melancholy oneself.

Why should we care about the expression of emotion in painting? One answer is that we just do place intrinsic value upon certain states of mind, such as repose, tranquillity, contemplation, excitement. But there are other considerations which are relevant to understanding the importance of expression.

Sometimes, if one has been caught up in selfish or trivial emotions, the vivid presentation of a noble or serene feeling has a tremendous impact. It certainly makes one aware of one's shortcomings. It also inspires and invigorates. One has the sense of returning to the true path.

Few terms have generated so much scholarly disagreement as the 'catharsis' that Aristotle says good tragedy produces in its audience. One way of understanding this term is as an emotional clarification. Suddenly the confusing and shifting play of emotions is set in order: one's real and important feelings are given prominence and authority. Daubigny's *Alders* remind us of the seriousness and inward calm that we are capable of feeling. This may induce a sense of relief: we recognise in such feelings our emotional home. It may also evoke a special pain: the pain in which the tawdry quality of much of our emotional life is recognised, how often we fail to live with our true concerns in sight. This pain is special because it is conjoined with a vision of self-understanding. We are emotional creatures; the education of our emotions matters to us.

We may also find that the press of the world is forever intruding upon our more sincere and valued emotional states. Calm lasts for a moment before something disturbs it – other people or a restless aspect of ourselves. A painting may preserve these emotions, allowing them to be entertained securely. A picture may perform this function for the painter too, which is why we should not be surprised if the emotional content of a work does not seem to cohere with the emotional character of the painter. A painter with an explosive, irritable temper may paint serene, generous works. This is not an act of hypocrisy. In painting, the painter is more able to secure the vivid realisation of emotions which elude him in daily living.

Notes

1. It is not merely that this makes it easier to see certain features of the works in question, features which could in principle have been seen without the aid of this notion. Suppose it is pointed out that Koch is working partly in the Greek style: this may lead one to see more easily that the textural simplicity of the etchings has an aesthetic point, and is not merely a matter of incompetence or lack of invention. This could be discerned without reference to the style of the work.

7

Myths and
Misunderstandings

1. Élitism

In the evening as the shadows deepen, objects seem to loose their individuality and are seen in broad clumps and soft groupings; the rose merges with the tree, the tree with the wall. So it is with twilight thoughts. It is hard to think in the broad daylight when powers of description are quickly overwhelmed by the precision of differentiation, when we are impelled to pick out the rose from the tree, the tree from the wall, when we must always be distinguishing and analysing.

It is a relief to fall back on the gentle generalities of twilight. We have seen this longing for shadowy ease: the mind resists having to work with two ideas when it could work with just one; it is sweet to let them merge into the cool, undifferentiated dusk.

I finally get to the large gallery at the rear of the building – I know that this is where the really great works are hung and the grand setting reflects their status: an expanse of dark polished parquet floor, tables set with bronze statues, the silk of the walls, the exquisite sofas on which no one is allowed to sit. The paintings are hung in two layers working their way high up the monumental walls, canvas after canvas of the highest possible quality, prime works of the prime painters: Rubens, Van Dyke,

Hals, Titian, Reynolds, Poussin, Claude, Velásquez. Just when excitement and pleasure should be gently enveloping me, a weariness creeps up, tired aches spread from my spine and chest, my eyes strain, I sit and look at the floor. Around this room a few people are strolling, pausing in their fine shoes and expensive clothes before the occasional painting, speaking quietly. A moment of anger rises up. For a moment, all these pictures seem to collude with the comfortable, the well off, the well fed, the leisured. They are paintings which in their excellence, their gracefulness, seem to be indifferent to the weak, the tired and the hard pressed.

Galleries like this sometimes encourage the charge that fine painting is 'élitist'. But what is the substance of this charge and, if it is a serious charge, is it one against which paintings of the kind discussed in this book can be successfully defended? The term 'élitist' used in an abusive sense is often rather vague, which from a rhetorical point of view adds to its effectiveness. It is a philosophical task carefully to separate the different threads which have become tangled together. In what follows I set out a selection of more specific complaints which may be launched under the charge of élitism. Of course, once a charge is made more specific it can be replied to: either we will find that it holds or it does not hold, and if it does hold we can evaluate whether this reveals something bad about fine painting.

The least interesting use of the term is as the mere expression of resentment. If I feel unable to participate in some activity which others are enjoying, I may deprecate that activity in order to console myself. Too shy and inhibited to dance at a disco, and envious of the rapture of those who do this so easily, I belittle the whole practice: this is a case of resentment. In another of its strands such belittling takes precisely the form of abusing the envied activity as élitist. My sense of exclusion is consoled by being politicised.

Another way of understanding the charge of élitism is this: a practice is élitist if it further advances those who are already advantaged. Reserving the best education for the offspring of wealthy families is, in this sense, élitist. The application of this more developed charge of élitism derives initial support from statistical studies of the people who go to art galleries. It is not only the bare number of visits to the gallery which are counted, but the kind of experience the visitor had there: did he feel comfortable in the gallery, did he feel that he could enjoy the paintings? The studies show that, with increasing education, and with increasing economic advantage, people have a better time in art galleries and go there more often. From these statistics someone might conclude that the objects which are in the galleries, the paintings themselves, encourage this profile of attendance, and are élitist.[1] Particular art forms have particular profiles at particular times. In general, fine painting is seen as a preserve. This can encourage the view that painting itself generates this preserve, this atmosphere of exclusion.

The truth is that people do use the arts in connection with social practice. Kant notes that the arts give people something to talk about. Exhibitions and galleries provide perfect dinner-party conversation; they provide tokens of belonging. 'We went to the Royal Academy/Sainsbury Wing/Tate.' This is perfectly packaged social chat.

However, from this social profile, which is what really generates the charge of élitism, nothing follows about the paintings themselves. The social profile takes its character not from the appreciation of the paintings, but from the use, or should one say abuse, of paintings for social life. It may have nothing to do with the paintings at all. One doesn't have to appreciate the paintings in order to like them or just look at them, or enjoy strolling round a gallery. And one can imagine many another thing playing the same role. It is the role, not the object, that constitutes the élitism in this case. The point is that the social facts which bolster this charge of élitism actually bypass the appreciation of painting. The social profile of painting has little to do with its appreciation. (The grounds of this distinction between appreciation and liking are discussed in Chapter 1.)

Even if this is granted, it might be pointed out that there is a further statistical investigation which concerns the social profile of those who *appreciate* fine paintings as works of art. So far as I know no such investigation has ever been carried out. Nevertheless, it is easy to imagine that those who appreciate them will broadly, but by no means exclusively, have economic and educational advantages. What are we to make of this?

Many activities have 'enabling conditions', conditions under which someone comes to be able to perform a task well. Suppose, for example, that in general Australians are better swimmers than people who live in Scotland. Part of the explanation will lie in the facts that the Australian government pays for swimming lessons for its citizens and that the water is warmer. But this does not show that swimming, as an activity, is biased towards people in Australia. What this example shows is that an activity can have a social profile (and be better carried out by a certain sector of the population) while that social profile really tells us very little about the activity itself. Suppose that (as was perhaps once the case) only those who could afford to go on holiday to the seaside would learn to swim. Swimming would then have a social profile which reflected economic advantage. But it is entirely obvious that swimming is not in itself an élitist practice. It may thus well be the case that those who are already advantaged are more likely to gain the further benefit of learning to appreciate paintings, but this does not show that there is anything in the appreciation of paintings which makes it an élitist activity.[2] That is, the appreciation of paintings cannot really be understood as a practice which gives further advantage to those who already have advantage.

At this stage, someone might introduce another way of understanding the term 'élitist', arguing that it is the very notion of 'appreciation' which is élitist. After all, they say, these pictures were made to advocate and celebrate the values of the patrons of the arts, people who in fact constituted the élite of past societies. The gracious Madonnas of Giovanni Bellini represent the Madonna as an upper-class woman (figure 17). The painter has insinuated a political value into the work: to hold the picture in high esteem is to give allegiance to the élitist values it embodies.

There are various ways one might respond to this. One could dispute it as an historical claim. Not all the works discussed were produced for an élite audience – but one would still have to concede that this was often the case. One might dispute that the content is the whole of what we appreciate. The upper-class Bellini Madonna can be appreciated for other features apart from her class: and the painting obviously offers us more than an attempt to align divine and social orders.

But the heart of the issue is this: it does not follow from the fact that a picture was produced for a patron of a certain class, a class which constituted an élite, that the work is itself élitist. The Bellini Madonna has universal virtues. She is calm, serious and tender as well as beautiful, she possesses a degree of simplicity without appearing naive. These are ideals which transcend the concerns of any particular class.[3] Suppose, then, that the patron for whom Bellini produced this work and who holds these values dear was a member of an élite Venetian family. There is nothing to prevent these values also being values which are held by members of other classes. If a value is transcendent (in that it goes beyond the considerations of any particular social class) then it is not surprising that some well placed patrons care for such values, but it does not mean that the values of calmness, seriousness and tenderness can be uniquely identified with a particular class.[4]

However, I think there remains one way in which the paintings discussed in this book may be properly described as élitist. Many paintings present the values they celebrate as worthwhile and important. In depicting the Madonna as serene, modest and contemplative, Bellini does not merely attribute these qualities to some woman, he holds them up as ideals of manner and disposition. He presents these as a vision of how a person should be. He presents a certain set of values as the right values, and by implication encourages us to turn from other ways of conducting ourselves. If we put a very high artistic value on a work such as this it is partly in virtue of the judgment that these are very worthwhile character traits to which Bellini has given form. One way of construing the term 'élitist' is as the claim that a particular set of values is the right set of values. In this sense, Bellini and every painter mentioned in this book are 'élitist'.

But it is by no means obvious that it is a bad thing to be élitist in this precise sense. Yet the vague use of 'élitist', which connotes injustice, is liable to predominate even here despite the fact that the precise form I have identified – holding a set of values to be right – cannot in itself be unjust. Indeed anyone who puts store by justice proclaims this – justice – as a value which it is right to hold to, and one which is superior to other values.[5]

2. The innocent eye and the educated eye

Experience has furnished us with expectations and associations which are alive in our visual perceptions. Some of these are general to the time. Any one of us would be surprised to see a street empty of cars and crowded, instead, with carriages and horses. To us, such a sight would be novel, confusing and interesting, whereas we generally regard a street lined with parked cars as the most boring and ordinary sight. To a nineteenth-century observer, the opposite would be true. The difference in the visual experience derives from difference in the experiences the spectators have had up to this point, which provide them with a set of expectations and anticipations. And it is relative to these expectations and anticipations that a scene is novel and interesting or familiar and dull.

Some perceptual baggage is private rather than general to the age. Charlotte associates the colour of the curtains with the water of Venetian canals. I have never been to Venice, and I associate the colour with goose excrement. To Charlotte it is an urban colour, sophisticated and romantic; to me it is rustic and slightly nauseating. Because we are furnished with these associations and expectations, it is said that our eyes are not 'innocent'. What the artist sees, the argument goes, depends upon his cultural and conceptual background, and the same is true of the spectator.[6] As we have each lost our innocence in an individual way, there can be no standard visual experience in regard to any particular object. It is no more right to have the associations Charlotte has than it is wrong to have the associations I have. And this point is hauled into the discussion of paintings: it is said that the beliefs and expectations which we bring to the picture determine how we see it and thus determine our response to the picture.

It cannot be doubted that our cognitive stock (of beliefs,

associations, anticipations and so on) *can* play an important role in our reactions to paintings. Say we are looking at Boudin's picture of Trouville (figure 20). We can vividly imagine the difference for someone who (living in the nineteenth century) saw nineteenth-century costume as *contemporary, fashionable, slightly outmoded* and such like. This contrasts with someone today who sees the costume as archaic and utterly removed from the norm. Surely, people say, this period eye must make a difference? We carry with us our presuppositions and expectations about dress, so we cannot see the picture as it was seen in the late nineteenth century. In this case the denial of the innocent eye is being used to support a claim about the impossibility of fully appreciating the work of the past. Or it is argued that because everyone has different expectations and presuppositions, a different history as a perceiving being, so each person sees the picture differently and there is no proper or right way to see it.

It is an unsupported dogma to insist that our expectations always colour our perceptions in every respect. Take an obvious example: when crossing the road we look out for traffic precisely without expectation, we are alert to danger, to the unexpected. This is a habit which we develop because it is the most reasonable approach to such situations if we want to take in what is important. We develop a habit of observation which is not dominated by expectations. Here we have a case in which a developed concern finds its way *past* expectations and prejudices, and away from the individual history. It is not that such a history disappears, far from it. It is just that that history is not mobilised in the perception. There is no reason at all why I should not develop a habit of perception in which, when looking at paintings, the nineteenth-century dress does not stand out as abnormal. It is not that my expectations have changed, it is just that my expectations do not dominate this perception. If I were to see someone on a real beach wearing such a costume I would think it highly eccentric. But when I look at a beach scene by Boudin, that expectation (that people wear modern dress) does not come into play. In this respect, the eye is educated.

The educated eye does not differ from the naive eye in that it has eliminated its expectations based on past experience. Rather, what has occurred is that within certain situations those associations (although we still have them) just do not apply; they do not engage with the task. The person who has learned to look carefully at the picture does not forget that this is not how people dress today: it is just that he has found something else to attend to which makes that bit of information irrelevant to the perceptual task in hand. It makes no impact upon his experience of the painting.

This phenomenon has a personal as well as an historical aspect. It is supposed – as is indeed the case – that everyone 'has their own associations'. This face reminds me of X. But as you have never seen X it cannot remind you of him. This colour reminds you of your first bicycle, but mine was red not blue. It may be supposed that these individualised clusters of association isolate one person's perceptual experience from another's, that 'we all see the world differently'. This lonely conclusion need not follow. Even if it is true that we have individual clusters of association it has not been properly argued that these do have the supposed consequence.

Our visual expectations often have their maximum impact upon our experience in unfamiliar and complex situations. Unable to comprehend so much detail in a brief time, we fall back upon habit to supply a structuring model, and this impregnates and guides what we are able to take in of the scene. Thus, when one walks into an unfamiliar room crowded with people and extravagantly decorated, it can be some time before one has anything like an accurate sense of the visual appearance of the room. In those first few minutes what I take in depends largely upon my perceptual history, and what Charlotte attends to and notices depends upon her different history. In this way, the room will look different to each of us, because we have attended to different aspects of it.

And something like this applies with respect to paintings. It takes more than a minute or two to see a painting even half properly, indeed merely to notice many of its details and subtleties of organisation can take a good deal longer than that. Take any work illustrated as an example of this. The task of fully grasping a painting is an open-ended one; there are relations between parts of the picture which have to be slowly digested: it takes time to grasp what a picture really looks like. Differences in what people see when they look at a picture, and especially when they look at it for a short period of time, do nothing to undermine the claim that there is a standard way it does look.[7] But the fact that people see different features of an object (a painting, a room) is compatible with there being a standard way the object looks (when seen from a certain spatial point of view).

The educated eye is not one which is devoid of associations or blank of expectations. It is one which knows when its associations and expectations are relevant and when they are not: it is not under the tyranny of the past, even though it is able, if need be, to draw upon the past; it has cultivated visual curiosity and attentiveness.

The notion of an educated eye is not unique to the discussion of painting. Suppose a surveyor is examining a building for dry rot. In his experience, a building of this type and age, and in this location is likely to be free from dry rot. But, if he is in the least good at his job, he is not going to fail to notice the signs of dry rot just because he does not expect them to be there. Attentiveness is obviously compatible with making use of past experience, but it requires that one's eye is not dominated by expectations derived from the past.

The possibility of an educated eye, an eye which has cultivated attentiveness, overturns objections to appreciation which are raised on the grounds that 'everyone sees things differently'. The fact that we are not innocent of expectation does not entail that there is no standard way things look. For our past experiences do not have to dominate our present observations, even though this *can* and sometimes *does* happen. But 'can' and 'do' are a world away from 'must', and the putative objection rests upon 'must'. Appreciation does not require what we cannot have, an innocent eye; it requires what we can cultivate: an educated eye.

3. Knowing and knowing-about

A classic discussion of the impact of information, or belief, upon perception occurs in John Berger's *Ways of Seeing*. His general claim is that what we see is greatly influenced by what we believe, or the information which we have about what we are looking at. Let me quote his description of an experience of looking at a painting by Van Gogh.

> Paintings are often reproduced with words around them. This is a landscape of a cornfield with birds flying out of it. *Look at it for a moment.* [There follows a reproduction of Van Gogh's *Wheatfield with Crows*.] Then turn the page. [Another illustration of the same work follows.] This is the last picture Van Gogh painted before he killed himself. It is hard to define exactly how the words have changed the image but undoubtedly they have. The image illustrates the sentence.[8]

Perhaps what Berger predicts will occur if one follows his instructions. What we have to put into question is what can be inferred from this result. The general view is that as our beliefs change our perception of the picture changes, and that our beliefs have their genesis independently of the picture and are imposed upon the picture.

One upshot of this view is as follows: the difference between appreciation and non-appreciation is cast in terms of beliefs. If I find a picture serene or dramatic this is because of what I believe about it and about its conditions of production. As Berger puts it, 'the picture illustrates the words'. There is then no way of testing the adequacy of the words to describe the picture. The beliefs always trump the picture. There is no way back, for the belief to be changed by the picture. In the Van Gogh case we want to allow the possibility that the sight of the picture should put into question the belief about the relation between the artist's state of mind and the perceived features of the object.

Yet Berger seems to have a point. If we do follow his advice the picture does seem to change. It is, I think, central to Berger's project that we look at the picture 'for a moment'. In that case, when we are presented with the shocking piece of news our perception is altered or influenced by the new belief. Contextual belief can then seem overwhelmingly important.

Imagine, by contrast, that one had been offered the original to take home for a few years, never learning that it was Van Gogh's last picture. One looks at it attentively, thinks about it from time to time in different moods, in different lights, at times of elation or depression or indifference. One might try to explain to others how one sees it, hear about their impressions and so on. After this period Berger tells us that this is the last picture Van Gogh painted before he committed suicide. Although I have not tried this experiment, I do think that the result would not be as shocking as the initial case presented by Berger. When one is well acquainted with the object it can be the case that a new belief, or new information, however piquant, does not influence the way we see the object. It has to take its place alongside our history of acquaintance and be measured against it. So we preserve the option of saying things such as 'Yes, I can well believe that', or 'How strange that this is not evident in the picture.'

Berger was able to make contextual belief loom large by describing a situation in which acquaintance was minimal. So there was nothing alongside which the contextual belief had to take its place, or against which it could be weighed. This may be the situation of the average gallery visitor, or it may not.

The belief that 'this was his last painting' is taken to generate a perceptual character for the work. But which character will depend upon a further belief about suicide and the state of mind of suicides, of the state of mind of Van Gogh as a suicide. What is the foundation for such belief? We simply are not entitled to *a priori* beliefs about the expressive content generated by the fact of suicide. In this case contextual belief is not revealing the picture but obscuring it. In the eyes of a naive viewer this sort of belief, without justification, comes to colour the perception and engender a crude mis-seeing. Not every true statement about the picture will help us to appreciate it, and such statements *may*, ironically, get in the way of appreciation. A statement may be true and have an impact upon the way we see a picture and yet be detrimental to appreciation. An example will make this point more vivid.

One of the most celebrated Pre-Raphaelite paintings is the *Ophelia* by John Everett Millais. The picture shows the drowned Ophelia lying face up in the water, faithful to Shakespeare's description

> There is a willow grows aslant a brook,
> That shows his hoar leaves in the glassy stream,
> There with fantastic garlands did she come,

to her 'muddy death'. Millais was scrupulously faithful to nature too, in the detailed representation of foliage and water. This scrupulousness extended to the representation of the young woman floating in the brook. Millais approximated this phenomenon by getting a certain Miss Siddal to lie (elegantly dressed) in a bath of water. Thoughtfully he kept the water warm with lamps. One day, however, he forgot to fill his lamps. The beautiful young woman contracted a serious illness following this exposure. This illness, and perhaps also her marriage to Dante Gabriel Rossetti, shortened her life.

This story is liable to dominate our perception of the picture, so that rather than seeing the tragic young woman who loved Hamlet we see poor Miss Siddal lying in a cold bath. But the story is only *liable* to do this. Given a wider understanding of paintings in general we are apt to disengage the facts of the story from our perception of the work of art.

4. Originality

'Originality' is widely used as a term of praise; if a work is said to exhibit originality this is often counted as a way of saying that it has high artistic value. But the term 'originality' is used in a variety of different ways. If we are to understand what the work is being praised for when it is praised *for* originality, we have to tease out the different ways in which the term can be employed.

Sometimes 'originality' is used with the implication that the work originates a movement or trend in subsequent painting. In this sense originality is like influence. This is often how the term is used with respect to twentieth-century art: a prime instance of originality would be a work which initiated a movement, or which inspired later artists. Thus we often hear a painter praised for having 'anticipated' some later movement.

In fact, there are very few cases, if any, in which a single work does clearly have this sort of impact. Most movements have many roots, not all of them artistic. But even supposing a work did have this sort of influence, this would not tell us much about its artistic value. It is just as possible that a work of mediocre or poor artistic value should have momentous effects on subsequent painting. The late eighteenth-/early nineteenth-century French painter Georges Michel is now largely forgotten and his works are not rated highly. He was, however, a decisive influence on the Barbizon school, a major movement of the mid-nineteenth-century which produced many fine works. Having influence does not itself suffice to make an artist great. Michel's work is original in the sense we are discussing. If 'originality' is understood as 'influential' then it is an inept term of praise with respect to artistic merit.

A second use of 'originality' is close to 'innovation'. This notion of originality does not connote subsequent influence: a work can be innovative without being influential. Again, a painting can be innovative without being artistically successful. Leonardo's *Last Supper* (plate 21), which we now see in a ruinous state, is an innovative work. One innovative feature concerns the placing of the Apostles: Judas is not isolated and sits in the same row as the other Apostles. Saint John does not lie on the Lord's breast, which was his traditional posture in such scenes. Clearly some other painter could have introduced these innovations (and perhaps did) a few years before Leonardo. It is clearly possible that such an innovation could have occurred in a mediocre or poor work.

Mere influence and mere innovation have nothing directly to do with artistic merit. Suppose now that a picture is influential because it uses an innovative feature *with great artistic success*. The point about *The Last Supper* is not merely that the Apostles are depicted in an innovative order, its importance lies in what Leonardo employs this innovation to achieve: an integration of disparate parts into a geometrically ordered unity. By making the position of the Apostles more regular, he can exploit a simple symmetry around the figure of Christ. And that symmetry is embellished by the dividing of each group of Apostles into two sub-groups of three. Clearly these formal concerns require that Judas is included with the other Apostles and that Saint John is kept at a distance from Christ. And the concern with the figures is continuous with Leonardo's formal concerns in the work as a whole. The arrangement of the depicted windows and ceiling, the whole perspectival order of the work, directs attention at the head of Christ.

This work displays originality in terms of the imaginative resource which Leonardo has brought to the organisation of the work as a whole. That is, he has conceived of a way of subordinating the narrative incident to the formal demands of the work as a whole. And these formal effects of symmetry and unity in turn give greater force to the narrative itself. The institution of the Blessed Sacrament is represented as a profoundly ordered event. The momentary confusion and agitation of the Apostles is utterly contained within an enduring and all-embracing order. That greater order is instantiated by the ordering power of the laws of perspective. If another painter had done all *that* a few years before Leonardo, then he would have painted a great work.

In a more general sense, 'originality' is used to ascribe imagination. When people use their imagination, by definition, they conceive of things in a way which is not routine, in a way which is 'original'. And this is a use which has application outside of discussion of the arts. A seducer, like the diarist of Kierkegaard's *Seducer's Diary*,[9] might display great imagination in the process of seduction. But in this case, the exercise of imagination is not praiseworthy. For what is done imaginatively in this case, the seduction and exploitation of an innocent young girl, is something which cannot be approved of; being 'highly imaginative' is not necessarily a virtue. The same holds for imagination with respect to painting. The seducer is over-rated by the seduced; the seducer may lavish imagination on ensuring this over-rating. A work may be highly imaginative, and yet the experience which we are invited by the work to have is not one which we can regard as being of high artistic value. Just as the experience which the seduced is invited to have is not one of high value: it is not real love. A painter may exercise great imagination in seducing the spectator into over-rating a trivial experience.

One of the social functions of art is to give us something to talk about. And for this, we require a set of interesting terms to keep the conversational furnace stoked. 'Originality' is perfect social fuel for chattering (which is not to deny that it can be used seriously). Conversational utility leads to the over-rating of the terms it finds useful: a case of the tail wagging the dog. Concepts which are of lesser importance from the point of view of artistic value (particularly 'innovation' and 'influence') have journalistic and conversational prominence. We transfer the conversational value to the level of artistic value (between which there is no real connection) and thereby come to the erroneous conclusion that innovation and influence are of the highest importance with respect to artistic value.

Notes

1. For details of such evidence and analysis of it, see John Berger, *Ways of Seeing*, BBC and Penguin Books, 1972, p. 24.

2. It is surely worth pointing out that the connection between economic and educational advantage and the appreciation of fine paintings as works of art cannot be a very strong one. Only a small proportion of the educated and well off have any interest in paintings, and many among these groups find themselves uncomfortable or bewildered in galleries.

3. In calling an ideal 'universal' I do not mean to imply that everyone holds it as an ideal. Rather, I mean that something like it is liable to be taken as an ideal across a wide range of social conditions.

4. This does not mean that class specific values are impossible. All I am pointing out is that premise one: the patron values tenderness, and premise two: the patron belonged to a social élite, do not entail the conclusion that tenderness is an élitist value. So one cannot successfully argue merely from the élite position of the patron to an élitism of the work.

5. Some people who advance their values as superior to all others are abominable. This naturally discredits the holding of values as superior. But, paradoxically, the person who says 'no one should proclaim his or her values as superior' is proclaiming yet another value as superior, the value of tolerance perhaps.

6. In *Art and Illusion*, Gombrich famously attacks what he calls the 'myth of the innocent eye'. The gist of his position is that perception necessarily involves interpretation, and interpretation depends upon the concepts which are employed in interpretation. This issue is not quite the same as the one I am discussing here. There is an important sense in which Charlotte and I see the same colour, only we have different reactions to it. In fact, I think it is at this level of *reaction* to what is seen, and not at the level of strictly *what* is seen (the level with which Gombrich concerns himself) that the important differences between individuals emerge.

7. A standard is relative to the particular distance and angle from which it is seen and the light in which it is seen.

8. John Berger, *Ways of Seeing*, pp. 27 and 28.

9. Søren Kierkegaard, *Either/Or*, translated by Alastair Hanny, Penguin Books, 1992.

8

Aesthetic Education

1. Ghastly good taste

Mademoiselle de Cambremer no longer loves Poussin, now
it is Degas and above all Monet whom she admires.

> 'But,' I said to her, feeling that the only way to rehabilitate
> Poussin in the opinion of Mlle. de Cambremer would be to
> tell her that he was once again fashionable, 'M. Degas
> insists that the Poussins at Chantilly are the most beau-
> tiful things he knows.'
>   'Really? I don't know the ones at Chantilly,' said Mlle.
> de Cambremer who didn't wish to disagree with Degas,
> 'but I can speak for those in the Louvre, they're horrible.'
>   'He also admires them enormously.'
>   'I must go and look at them again. My memory of them
> is rather vague,' she replied after a moment of silence, as
> if the favourable judgment which she would soon have of
> Poussin would depend not on what I had just told her but
> on the additional and this time definitive examination to
> which she intended to submit the Louvre pictures.[1]

As Proust's passage bears witness, there can be change of
taste without development of taste. Mlle. de Cambremer's
somersaults of taste are not the result of a deepening
appreciation; she no more appreciates Degas now than she
will soon appreciate Poussin. In both cases her preference,
her taste, is founded on a whim of fashion, not on a real
valuing of the object on its intrinsic merits.[2]

It goes without saying that a person's preferences, when

it comes to paintings, change over time. Among these *changes*, are there some which, unlike those Proust describes, count as *developments* of taste?

Why should we think that development of taste is possible? Hindsight, as we survey the history of our affections, allows that past attachments may be comprehended as they are surpassed. Pascal tells the story of the Roman soldier who, in the sack of Athens, sees an old man scratching in the dust, and strikes him down. The old man is Archimedes; to the soldier the elegant geometrical proof is mere tracing in the dust. Archimedes, Pascal reflects, could understand the soldier, but the soldier could not understand Archimedes. In turn, Pascal supposes that he can comprehend Archimedes although Archimedes would have found the *Pensées* baffling; there is a hierarchy of development in which each higher stage comprehends those which preceded it. So too, we may think, with the development of taste. When Charlotte, whose taste is now for Vermeer and Chardin, looks back on her adolescent liking for Monet she need not think 'what a fool I was'. She may now understand what it was about Monet that attracted her adolescent self; although as an adolescent she could not appreciate Vermeer or Chardin, painters whose subtlety of mood eluded her girlish notice. She compares her baby self, who cared exclusively for a knitted rabbit called Podge, with the Roman soldier of Pascal's parable.

A retrospective sense of development cannot be taken for granted as an automatic self-approval, ready always to sanction whatever changes occur as development. There is a vein of honesty which allows that we may see our taste not as developing but as contracting, our engagement with works of art becoming less intimate, less satisfying. Self-approval is hard to come by, though the public surface may suggest the opposite.

It is evident that the parable of development does not apply to Mlle. de Cambremer; although she would be the last to recognise this. Suppose in the next volume Marcel tells her that Degas is no longer fashionable, and true to form Mlle. de Cambremer finds that she loathes Degas. She would be in no position to understand, and continue to care about, what it was that attracted her to Degas in the first place. There is no sense here of a development of taste, only a shifting from one invented preference to another.

The comprehension of past taste by present taste gives one reason why we should allow for development, as opposed to mere change, of taste; another, equally personal, reason is provided by the private turning point in our relation to a particular work. After gazing for a while at Titian's *Bacchus and Ariadne* (plate 22) without much enthusiasm, one may begin to see how the gesture of Ariadne echoes that of Bacchus, how the vibrant physical expressiveness of their gestures is taken up in the contortions of the Bacchantes; one begins to savour the heavy, saturated colours and the sense of dusk and the enclosed night-mystery of the woods. A transition is experienced from dull incomprehension to a lively, sensuous and immediate *rapport* with the picture. This dawning (if and when it happens) is the sense of coming to appreciate, of appreciation developing; before one could not appreciate, now appreciation is possible.

Private life, in retrospect and in the moments of dawning, furnishes us with the conviction that taste can develop and not merely change. The recognition that some kinds of taste are more developed than others and qualitatively superior is at the top of a slippery slope declining gently to smugness and condescension, precipitously to contempt and brutality. Yet slippery slope arguments on their own do not show us that something should be rejected, simply on the grounds that it could have dangerous consequences if we are not careful; rather, they sound the call to be careful. Besides, heartfelt taste develops freely and cannot be forced.

From what has been said so far, it may be thought that a hierarchy of *objects* is proposed, with Mlle. de Cambremer's watercolour sketches at one end and the *Mona Lisa* at the other with every painting ranked somewhere in between. Taste develops, according to this Dantesque vision, as one's affections ascend the great chain of works.

But this is not in the least the suggestion. Instead, what is of primary importance, and what develops as taste develops, is the quality of *relation* to the picture. Appreciation comes by degrees; I may like a work although I appreciate it but little. What I mean by a development of taste is a development of appreciation. Mlle. de Cambremer prefers, for today, Monet to Poussin; she does not appreciate Monet any more than she appreciates Poussin. Each of those painters gives us so much to appreciate, there is so much space in each for us to grow into, that a development in our appreciation could be witnessed by a shift in preference from P to M or from M to P. A connoisseur may find that the summit of his career as a lover of painting is a full and deeply perceptive appreciation of a comparatively minor painter.

Some pictures do offer us finer and more profound things to appreciate than others; as taste develops there is a tendency to home in on these greater things. But the personal history of development need not replicate the scale of greatness, and will in any case be made up of wide circuitous wanderings, false starts, back tracking and returns.

Being what we are, growth in our capacity to appreciate is accompanied by a change in the object of interest. At first, delighting in bright tones and happy incidents, Charlotte is attracted to the paintings of Claude Monet. Then her concern grows for narrative and romance: she is attracted to the Pre-Raphaelites; then she comes to be more appreciative of composition, her preferences turn, for a while, in another direction, towards Poussin and Raphael. As she comes also to appreciate evocation of mood, her taste undergoes a further shift, to Titian first, then Vermeer and Chardin.

This history of development depends on emphasising the quality of relation above the objective value of the painting. We do not say that Charlotte's taste has developed because Chardin is a better painter than Monet, her first love. Her development cannot be traced in terms of the preferred pictures occupying progressively higher rungs on a scale of pictorial excellence. The claim, equally, cannot be that someone has good taste merely because she likes Titian.

Although someone goes for the fine and the refined, her relation to it may be crude and simplistic, as was seen with Mlle. de Cambremer. This person does not have a relation of high appreciation to the picture, although she likes a painting which could sustain a rich appreciation.

Confusion threatens if we fail to admit this distinction between the quality of the picture and the quality of the enthusiast's relation to the picture, and to see its implications. For this distinction explains the hollowness of art snobbery. Art snobbery is the lauding of attachment to works that hold a high place in the scale of greatness, merely because they hold such an exalted place. But we have seen that someone could be attached to the finest works and have little appreciation of them. The splendour of her object choice confers, in this case, little splendour on her. Snobbery, and not just art snobbery, arises not from the hierarchy of value, not because one thing is better than another; it arises from the fact that the real hierarchy of value can be abused.

The distinction between the greatness of the picture and the quality of the viewer's relation to it also explains why art snobbery is not an indictment of art; it is merely an indictment of our capacity to have shallow relations to profound objects, to be unappreciative of what we could appreciate.

2. A note on self-deception

'Mademoiselle de Cambremer deceived herself over the refinement of her taste; could it not be that you also deceive yourself, and that what is paraded as the development of taste is no more than a flattering delusion which dresses up mere change of preference in the guise of "development" and "refinement"?'

It is the height of delusion to suppose that one never deceives oneself; but it is madness to spy the shadow of self-deception everywhere. 'Perhaps,' says the madman, 'I deceive myself in thinking that I deceive myself, or is this too self-deception; all is deception, even this thought.'

Thus is revealed one move against the possibility of universal self-deception: it is self-defeating. The very notion of self-deception only comes into play against a larger background, and that larger background must be one which includes the real possibility of not deceiving oneself. The best support that can be offered for the claim that taste can develop is a description of how it develops, a tracing of the process whereby people may come to have a more appreciative relation to the pictures they like. What is required in order to appreciate a painting, or more broadly, to appreciate paintings? What capacities does a person need to cultivate in order to appreciate painting pursued as an art?

The next section traces the history of a part-fictional, part-real aesthetic education: that described by Proust in *Remembrance of Things Past*. This novel may be seen as standing in the tradition of the *Bildungsroman*. This literary tradition, or institution, recognises the narrative and plotted nature of human development: full of reversals and unexpected turns. Difficulties, even seeming disasters, can foster a self-awareness and fortitude which go on to be crucial to later achievement. Reversals and recognitions are woven, as we hope them to be in life, into an intelligible and sustaining sequence. The novelistic structure is perfectly suited to the history of individual developments.

It is true that the history of development we are contemplating, that described by Proust, is exceptional, even freakish. This is a life in which devotion to art and aesthetic experience of nature plays an unusually important role, some may want to say too great a role. But for present purposes this is an advantage: in this narrated life the process of development is unusually clear and we can see magnified in the extreme version what is much harder to discern in ordinary life.

3. Remembrance of Things Past

The imaginative response

One of the roots of Proust's aesthetic sensibility has already been mentioned, in Chapter 4, when the description of his rapt attention to sunlight falling on a stone contemplated during a childhood walk was quoted.

> ... suddenly a roof, a gleam of sunlight on a stone, the smell of a path would make me stop still, to enjoy the special pleasure that each of them gave me, and also because they appeared to be concealing, beyond what my eyes could see, something which they invited me to come and take but which despite all my efforts I never managed to discover .... I would concentrate on recalling exactly the line of the roof, the colour of the stone, which, without my being able to understand why, had seemed to me to be bursting, ready to open, to yield up to me the secret treasure of which they were themselves no more than the lids.[3]

At the end of this passage a note of dissatisfaction is sounded: the objects promise something which is not delivered, they offer the prospect of satisfaction but this remains unfulfilled. There is pain when the object slips not only from sight but from imaginative sight; like an insight which is held for a moment only before it cools, and with it vanishes a glimpsed consolation.

The will to appreciate is there, and this must speak to everyone who wants to appreciate painting, but the will is frustrated: the child cannot make the object come alive even though the first impression was brimming with life. His relation cannot take on a broad and fructifying character: it remains a tantalising frustration. The rest of the novel can be seen as an attempt to trace a route from the first intimation of such satisfaction to the eventual possession of this promise.

Shortly after this a related experience is described. The young Marcel has been offered a seat on the top of a carriage belonging to the local doctor. This new point of view startles him into attention. His is struck by the evening light on the towers of a local church, bathed in a pink light, and by the manner in which the tower of a more distant church suddenly seems close by, by some transformation of the aerial perspective.

Marcel writes about what he has seen. The point is not merely that he records what he has seen, much more that he tries to do something with his impressions. His description is itself an attempt to produce an aesthetically satisfying object, an attempt to respond to, and do something with, what he has seen.

This is a point of the widest implications. But it is also vulnerable to misunderstanding. In its simplest terms, the claim is this: it is in the attempt to create a responding object that we begin to develop our capacity to appreciate the thing responded to.

But perhaps as so stated the claim is too strong; it

cannot be a necessary condition for appreciation that one go on to try to produce a corresponding work. Marcel's attempt illuminates a more basic problem: how we can attempt to hold on imaginatively to our experience? For only in so holding on, and holding on in a way which remains at the aesthetic level, can we overcome the problem of fleetingness.

It would be too much if the appreciation of natural beauty required each person to write their own *Remembrance*, although this has a certain appeal. But whatever the truth of that, we can take the hint about what counts *towards* appreciation, what partly constitutes appreciation.

The hint is that our effort of re-creation, of imaginative exercise, of trying to make use of the impression and the feeling it arouses and trying to do this artistically, is part of the appreciation of the work; it is part of the capacity to appreciate.

To switch back to painting, what is so distinctive of the Impressionists is not, as already noted, their intense response to light, but how they work their response into their own paintings. Others had responded to light; before them no painter had done so much *with* light. And we can give much less exalted descriptions of a response persisting in someone's life. It lives in his imagination, in his repertoire of references, it stands in the endless chain of comparisons and interactions with new images and objects; it is tried on, as it were, in diverse situations, it is called upon to feed responses to other things.

This is a capacity which is not fostered, although neither is it hindered, by extensive knowledge *about* a picture. Someone could spend his life memorising facts about paintings and never develop the capacity to make an image count in his imaginative and emotional life. Such a person would lack a major condition for the appreciation of painting practised as an art.

The impact of others

A further step in Marcel's aesthetic education comes in his conversations with Elstir, a fictitious painter who seems at times to have been modelled on Degas, at others on Monet or even Boudin.

On his first journey to the Normandy resort he calls Balbeck, Marcel is filled with romantic dreams about the stormy coast, wreathed in mist and echoing with the cries of the Cimmerians, the mythical ancient people of the farthest West. When he gets there, of course, he finds the world of early twentieth-century beach fashion: ladies in yachting dresses, sunshine, tourists, cars. In his discussions with Elstir, the painter shows him, with words and pictures, how to see what beauty there is in these scenes; he describes the aesthetic attractions of the racecourse:

> There's that peculiar creature, the jockey, on whom so many eyes are fastened, sitting there in the paddock gloomy and grey-faced in his bright jacket, reigning in the rearing horse that seems to be one with him; how interesting it would be to study his professional movements with the bright splash of colour and the horse's coat blending in, all against the background of the course! What a transformation of every visible object in that luminous vastness of a race course where everyone is constantly surprised by the fresh lights and shades which you only see there. How pretty the women can look too![4]

Elstir picks out details: the expression and pallor of the jockey's face, the neatness of his movements; these a quick glance might miss. He points to relations and ensembles: the movements of rider and horse, the contrast between face and jacket, the counterpoint of the attention of the crowd and the self-absorption of the jockey. He reveals its aesthetic order, the order of its special light and open vastness, and allows Marcel to see this too. The appreciation spirals outwards: from seeing the aesthetic point of the racecourse, Marcel can go on to see the charm of the fashionably dressed women. He can see how things go together to form a stylistically coherent whole. Although this starts from the words of another it gathers the force of personal experience.

Getting a joke is not merely a matter of believing that the joke is funny. Finding a joke funny is a whole further realm which lies apart from the belief about the joke. A sense of humour can be encouraged by things people say, even when what they say isn't itself funny. *Comique professionel* derives from the fact that although the professions obviously exist for public benefit any profession can only justify its higher flights of pride in supposing that the public exists for it. This is not itself an amusing point, but it may serve to open one's eyes to a whole range of humour: it is a principle of Molière's wit. 'A dead man is only a dead man,' says one of Molière's doctors, 'but a neglected formality brings the entire professional body into disrepute', while another doctor notes that 'it is better to die according to the rules than to get well against the rules'.[5] What Elstir is doing is the aesthetic equivalent of getting the rather sober Marcel to see the joke.

There is an exact parallel with this in the work of the finest critics. They induce us into a mood of receptiveness, they foster in us the attitudes or excitements which are important if we are to see the point of certain work, if we are to have feeling for it. They encourage, as it may be, a love of stone and of the working of stone; they bring us, as it were, into the community in which we can get the joke, or see the point. It is in fostering our aesthetic humour that the real contribution is made.[6]

'But if he could come to like that, he could come to like just any thing.' Perhaps, but this is not to the point. For Marcel's taste has not developed merely because Elstir has induced a change in his imaginative attachments.

Some changes in imaginative attachment may be for the worse, coarsening and cheapening taste.

Consider a parallel in terms of people. Say that for a while I have been wary of X, but on developing acquaintance find that I really rather like X – this does nothing to show that I could become friends with just anyone. The mistake perhaps has this explanation. Presupposing that Marcel could have liked just anything, if only it were favourably described, would make it unsurprising that he came to like Balbeck under Elstir's guidance. But this is not the only possible explanation.

One of the perennial problems of a sceptical age is the power it gives to the sardonic. For it is presupposed that the argument which undercuts is right, the more cynical the conclusion the less it really needs to be argued for; it speaks for itself. Of course this has its uses, but it is a net which entangles some of the most elegant and spirited of our attachments.

How should we describe what is going on when Elstir influences Marcel? Elstir tries to direct Marcel's eyes and attention in a situation which is unfamiliar. This is like learning to ride a bicycle. When you are on the bicycle struggling to keep it going, the things people shout, such as 'Turn the handle bar, keep pedalling', can be helpful. But no one would try to teach abstract 'bicycle theory' without getting on a real bicycle and having a go. Or if they did they would not succeed in teaching anyone to ride.

The features of a picture, like its gracefulness, delicacy, bold design, balance, are things which we want to see for ourselves. Although there are no simple rules for the achievement of these features, or qualities, we can admit that they are dependent upon the material features of the picture which anyone can see.

This point, about the process of learning to appreciate, draws together a number of themes which have been running through the book. For example, the difference between knowing and knowing about a painting. It is not that the latter cannot contribute to the former; of course it can. The point is that they are distinct and that knowing the painting is more important than knowing about it. And this comes home when we think about the process of learning to appreciate. Because, after all, knowing about a painting can proceed perfectly well in the absence of the picture itself, or with a poor reproduction. Now we see that acquiring the skill of appreciation aims at something which 'knowing about' cannot achieve. As in the case of the bicycle: you could be an expert about bicycles and yet not have acquired the skill of riding a bicycle. So too with art: the intrinsic value of painting can only be appreciated in experience – and it is that kind of experience we need to learn to cultivate. One needs to know about the picture – but the point of this knowledge is the way it can be put to use in the service of perception.

4. Contingency and permanence

Proust makes great play with the associations which are part of our experience, and enjoyment, of objects; he is a poet of associations. A painting is sometimes the starting point for our associations which play pleasantly through our mind as we look. A smell may bring back a forgotten period of life, a person; a set of attitudes and aspirations well up in the wake of the scent. Colours and images may do this too. So certain textures of paint bring back the dining room of childhood where a warmly coloured painting of a bowl of flowers hung. That picture has the power to evoke things which surrounded it: the view from the window, the texture of the carpet, and the table, and less tangible things like the moods of childhood afternoons, periods of waiting and loneliness.

But how contingent those associations are! They belong uniquely to me, and their reawakening depends upon chance: the chance that another object will present me with just that sense of texture and colour and bring back the immediacy of recollection.

One cannot really give away the story of *Remembrance of Things Past*. The climax of the novel, which is prefigured at many earlier points and prepared in many details, comes on the afternoon late in his life when Marcel listens to a piece of chamber music performed at a social party. The point about art, he begins to realise, is that its relation to our responses is not contingent. In some ways it is *like* the contingent evocation of the sound of a spoon striking against a plate or the feel of a starched napkin, sensations which, like Charlotte's perfume, serve to awaken a host of recollections. Music transforms sound, just as a painting may transform what is visible, deliberately. In this way the possibility opens for an escape from contingent attachment. Not so much an escape from contingency, but a securing of response, a preservation in an object altogether more durable and protecting.

The work may provide, for cherished feelings, for feelings which the tumble of the world is apt to knock about, a haven where they may be preserved, and with them a part of ourselves is preserved. The price of doing this is that our feeling for the work is not contingent. If it were, as Proust points out, we might go through life and never strike the right sound.

For example, suppose we think that Chardin has a specific private response to certain textures and colours, perhaps the very ones we see depicted and presented in one of his works. The question at once arises 'What is that to me?' It is with this question that the whole problem of the relation between my private history and the public object comes alive. Why should Chardin's emotional responses to cloth and colour move me? How can it be that it doesn't matter whether ochre or velvet have ever mattered to me, that I find in this picture something of the immediate attachment which (in other circumstances) private connection evokes?

And this throws up one of the deepest problems in the discussion of appreciation and the value of art. For a start, when we value something (or have a value) we do not take it that it is unique to us – we have to think of it as a value transcending our particular appreciation – that is, as part of what it is for something to be held valuable.

This is also tremendously liberating, for it means that the value of the object is not dependent upon us, and therefore will not suffer from an act of disloyalty. Think here of the possibilities of hysterical defensiveness if one supposed that a value really did depend upon one's own attachment to it.[7]

Three facets of aesthetic education have been contemplated. The first was imaginative yearning and the consequent resonance an image can have in imaginative and emotional life. The second was the role of others in leading the eyes, in cultivating the sense of what to look at and how to look, a sense which is neither prescriptive nor conventional. The third concerned the play between private associations and the grasp that a great work transcends these associations.

These capacities do not suffice for appreciation. They serve to illustrate some human potentialities relevant to the appreciation of painting, capacities of sensibility and imagination, of investment and self-transcendence. These can be cultivated but not forced. In their absence engagement with painting is liable to be a sterile and conventional affair, and loveless. The capacities cited do not displace the need for knowledge about a painting, nor for an awareness of the artist's employment of the resources of the art-form; the appreciation of the work of art is a complex process taking something from each.

5. Farewell to the spectator

The appreciation of painting is an activity, or process, which has resonance in life beyond the time we actually spend looking at particular works. This means that, in the end, a full appreciation of the value of art will involve transcending the role of mere spectator. Throughout this book the active participation of the spectator has been emphasised: the active spectator contains the embryonic artist.

When this embryo does not develop (and we shall have to become clearer about what its development involves) we are left with a stunted being: the 'celibate' of art. This is the spectator who is cut off from his own artistic capacities, who is most likely to say 'I have no talent'. As if by compensation, this spectator is likely to be settled in a devotion to art. As Proust describes it: they long for flight, but they have not worked out how to use their wings. Enjoying the flight of others is a very mixed admiration; not really a substitute for flying oneself. There is a painful irony here, that the most 'official' aspect of appreciation is liable to be the one that is prone to this celibacy; thus it is set at a distance from the full engagement with art.

But what is this further feature, this transcendence of the role of spectator? It need not be so literal as the taking of brush or pen in hand and the creation of autonomous works. The real matter is that one should proceed for oneself with the task of the 'translation' of experience. This 'translation' amounts to the piecing together of the different strands of experience: it is the business of self-knowledge. What has really mattered to me, and why did it matter? What has gripped my attention, and why did it affect me that way? This may produce surprising results: it may be that the recollection of sunlight on a simple wall, or shadows extending beneath trees by the bank of a swift river, are more important than sumptuous or raucous parties, so much heralded in public. This evaluation of experience is something we can do only for ourselves, and it is something which the good artist does in the process of working.

This task is essentially an artistic undertaking. For it concerns a perceptiveness towards the details of experience and the discernment of the underlying themes of experience. This is not, indeed, what every artist sets out to do, but it is, nevertheless, the central and abiding artistic undertaking.

The quality of our relation to pictures cannot finally be divorced from the seriousness of our self-examination and our attentiveness to experience outside the gallery and outside the studio. In the pursuit of an appreciation of painting we are led, finally, to transcend our fascination with art. We turn to the contemplation of what it was that originally moved the artists we care for: the pleasures and mysteries of ourselves and the world.

6. Wholeness

Life conspires to fragment us. The demands of practical living, our concern with what is useful and sensible may conflict with our desires. But it can also conflict with our understanding. We can be at odds with ourselves because we yearn for something finer or more sustaining than our life seems to yield. This is as real a conflict as that between good sense (call it reason, as has often been done) and sensuous desire – the desire to eat and drink too much, to flirt recklessly, to seduce without care, to lie idle. Our sensuous appetites, our practical wisdom, our imagination and spirituality and our powers of understanding and love of explanation thus hem in and interrupt one another. Divested of imagination, practical good sense degenerates into routine and philistinism; separated from sensuality, intelligence grows cold; spirituality cut off from understanding is in danger of falling into eccentricity.

At its best painting allows for, in fact demands, a response which reintegrates these capacities and diverse aspects of nature; this is something some painters have been able to do with paintings. It does not represent a declared aim, and there are many fine works which do not rise to this, but many do. We have seen, in the discussion of specific paintings, and in following the trajectory of the development of taste, how the appreciation of a painting as a work of art often involves that we respond to it emotionally and with sensual pleasure. We have to feel and we have to be sensitive to colour and line, but also we have to understand the structure of the work, we have to grasp the content and we have to evaluate intellectually the worth of certain contents. This is a process which involves bringing together just those qualities which, for the most part, daily life often keeps apart. Equally, we must not think that such rewarding experience could arise automatically as one stares hopefully at a picture. That just does not happen.

7. The place of the love of art in life

Is a concern with the arts good for us? Let us look to experience, says Kant, 'for this shows that connoisseurs in taste not only often, but generally, are given up to idle, capricious and mischievous passions, and that they could perhaps make less claim than others to any superiority of attachment to moral principles'.[8] Art is seductive: it entices our interest away from reality and furnishes us with respectable but diverting fantasies; it encourages us to wallow in emotions which are not our own.

There is something gratuitous about paintings: we will get by without them. And to a person of a certain pragmatic cast of mind those who devote their lives to the production and enjoyment of such things are not to be taken seriously; how could they be when what they do doesn't matter?

If some works of art are valuable, and do matter seriously, it is still possible to overrate their importance; the aesthete is someone who overrates the value of art. The attempt to judge all things in life – ideas, actions, character – by the standards of art, is bound to fail. The more elegant line of thought is not thereby the more rationally persuasive; a graceful action may be callous; the piquant or vivid personality may be untrustworthy or foolish. The overestimation of the importance of art is a deformation of life, like many other overestimations: of the importance of making money or satisfying sexual longings or playing golf. The fact that some people give art too exalted a place does not indicate that it should have no place in life; any more than the tragedy of living merely for sexual excitement casts any doubt on the value of sexuality.

To care for art above goodness and truth is to do an injustice to art: it is often to fail to appreciate what the artists themselves are calling us to care about.

There used to be (and still is) a phenomenon of 'good ordinary painting'. That is, work by painters not of the first rank which all the same demonstrates many virtues of technical excellence and pictorial competence: which is, in short, a good professional job. There must be as there are in all things which involve skill, a place for the recognition of acquired professional competence, which, while perhaps not achieving the heights, is far above the work of the amateur. This includes the sort of finesse which comes with experience. Such work offers a good deal to the appreciative eye: while not of the first rank it may still offer aesthetic satisfaction.

It has been noted often enough that although the great galleries of the world give us the chance to see work of the highest quality, they generally do so in an atmosphere which is detrimental to appreciation. Appreciation takes time, but it also takes variation in mood – sometimes one needs to be relaxed or open to a certain sort of melancholy or wistfulness or slowness – some works are best seen when one feels light and energetic, or spirited with an appetite for pleasure. How often – to put only the simplest of these demands – does one feel that response would come much more easily if one could view the picture after dinner, or early in the morning, sitting in a comfortable chair, sometimes in pure light and at other times in shadow. In themselves these are, individually, imperfect conditions for appreciation, nevertheless they stimulate the imagination and one returns to the picture with an added trace of attention, so that full appreciation later makes use of insights grasped at those propitious moments. Literally and metaphorically, to appreciate a work fully we need to live with a picture and to get to know it, to see it close up, move it about and so on.

While for most people that is not possible with work of the first rank, it is (much more widely) available in regard of good ordinary painting. For it is possible for far more people to have intimate relations to such work.

Notes

1. Marcel Proust, *Remembrance of Things Past*, vol. 5, *Sodome et Gomorrhe*, Gallimard Folio edition, pp. 207-8. My translation.

2. The term 'taste' is used in at least two quite distinct ways. First, it is used as a synonym for 'preference'. In this sense each person has his own taste. Secondly, it is used to signal a standard. We say that a joke is 'tasteless' or in 'bad taste', meaning that it falls below a standard of propriety and tact, a standard which we take to be important. In this sense someone can fail to have taste, or have bad taste, whether they realise it or not.

3. Marcel Proust, *Remembrance of Things Past*, vol. 1, translated by C.K. Scott Moncrieff and Terence Kilmartin, Penguin, p. 195.

4. Marcel Proust, *Remembrance of Things Past*, vol. 2, *A l'ombre de jeunes filles en fleures*, Gallimard Folio edition, p. 495. My translation.

5. I follow Bergson's discussion of Molière: see Henri Bergson, *Le rire*, Presses Universitaires de France, ch. 1, pt. 3.

6. One excellent exponent of this sort of critical enthusiasm (T.S. Eliot calls the class 'critics with gusto') is Adrian Stokes: see *The Stones of Rimini*, London, 1934.

7. The intersubjective validity of statements about value is one of the most contested issues in philosophy. In order to avoid these treacherous waters I consider the matter separately in an appendix.

8. Kant, *Critique of Judgment* §42.

Appendix

A Universal Voice

This appendix is in two parts. Both are concerned with the same question: can judgments about artistic value be valid for all? The first, sections 1 – 3, pursues its answer at the level of conversation. In the second part, section 4, I try to translate the answer into more conventionally philosophical prose. This has the advantage of allowing greater argumentative precision and rigour. But it has a price: the reader cannot be treated with much courtesy, and for some readers this will be reason enough to leave it aside. I would like to think that these different styles of writing complement one another.

1. Justifying judgments about value

One of the great rug-pulling exercises of the present century has been to say that – in spite of our instincts – our evaluations can be *explained away*. Despite what I am inclined to say – so the line goes – *in fact* I like Corot's *Avignon* (plate 1) because I went to Avignon at an impressionable age and this picture reminds me of the happiest of family holidays, add to this the fact that my father admires Corot's sketches. The conclusion which gets drawn is that I think this is a great painting *because* I am influenced by my parents and because I have a personal link with its subject matter. There are of course many variations on this rug-pulling business; a sociological version might insist that I like this picture because I am middle-class and it is the sort of thing middle-class people like. My background, it is claimed, has 'conditioned' my taste.

This sort of manoeuvre is taken to *explain away* the value of the picture. It is not that the Corot is a fine painting, but there are social or personal factors which make some people say that it is a great painting. This *explaining away of value* is endemic in contemporary life.

2. The overestimation of difference

That taste (preferences and loves in the arts, such as mine for Corot's oil sketches) is nothing more than a subjective attachment is one of the best believed dogmas of the age: it is both orthodox and popular. My attachment to Avignon is to be explained with reference to things particular to me and my history, not by way of the good qualities of the picture which I appreciate. The partner of this dogma is an absolute and final conviction that it is utterly impossible for a value judgment, such as the judgment that *Avignon* is a fine and beautiful work, to be justified and right – which would entail that someone who didn't like it would be in error. Why is this conviction so strong?

After a fashion, it all begins with Egyptian pigs. In his unflappable way Herodotus tells us what he thinks we ought to know (he is capable of phrases such as: 'I know the origins of this practice, but do not think it seemly to say what they are') about the pig in Egypt:

> Pigs are considered unclean. If anyone touches a pig accidentally, he will at once plunge into a river, clothes and all, to wash himself; and swineherds though of pure Egyptian blood are the only people in the country who never enter a temple, nor is there any intermarriage between them and the rest of the community ...[1]

It is quite clear, according to Herodotus, that pigs are not really unclean: it is only a local curiosity of the Egyptians to think so. The sincerity of their conviction, and the extent to which they let it guide their lives are in no way related to the conviction being justified or true. It does not require much imagination to move from the observation that a neighbour's convictions, however intense, may be false, to the recognition that one's own convictions may be false no matter how intense they are. We stand face to face with doubt: may it not be that my conviction about the excellence of the Corot landscape is just the same as the ancient Egyptian conviction about the pig?

The *unclean pig* model is one we might think best explains judgments about artistic quality; and, in fact, this is the model most people subscribe to these days. Unless we give in to majoritarianism, however, this body of agreement proves nothing.

At this stage it is important to be clear about the state of the argument. A model (that of the *unclean pig*) has been presented, and it is suggested that it applies in the case of judgments about artistic quality (a judgment that a picture by Corot is artistically valuable is like a judgment that pigs are unclean). But if the claim is to stick it must be proved that this *is* the right model for judgments about artistic quality.

Coming out of court a successful defendant might crow: 'My innocence has been proven,' he shouts. Not so, his guilt has not been proven, and that is quite a different matter. It is still possible that he perpetrated the crime and is, in fact, guilty. In court a verdict of *not proven* is obviously important, and obviously different from proof that someone is innocent. In our discussion, I shall simply try to show that the charge that judgments about artistic quality are merely subjective (a curious fact about me, on the unclean pig model) is not proven.

Here is the case for the defence. Nothing has been done to *show* that differences in judgments about artistic quality *must* be understood on the unclean pig model. One major impetus to the conclusion that they should be is that differences of taste do not seem like factual disagreements; mediaeval geographers thought that the earth was flat but they just got it wrong, however poetic their error. There are fully satisfactory procedures for proving that the earth is not flat; there are no fully satisfactory ways of proving that a little oil sketch by Corot is a fine painting.

However, the fact that a particular model of proof (that suited to claims of fact) does not fit judgments of artistic quality is not on its own sufficient to justify the conclusion that such judgments are the equivalent of the conviction that pigs are unclean. One thought ought to give us pause. There is a tendency for judgments about artistic excellence to transcend differences:

> For when men who differ in their habits, their lives, their enthusiasms, their ages, their dates, all agree together in holding one and the same view about the same writings, then their unanimous verdict, as it were, of such discordant judges makes our faith in the admired passages strong and indisputable.[2]

There is a substantial body of work of which this point is true. This observation effectively undermines any attempt to explain away judgments of excellence by reference to the particular situation of the person making the judgment.

This example casts doubt on the explaining away technique (enshrined in the *unclean pig* model of judgment). Pointing to the variety of circumstances under which similar judgments are made undermines the suggestion that it is the circumstances and not the object which explain the judgment. And the whole thrust of the 'explaining away' technique is to say that it is the circumstances – class, upbringing, etc. – and not the object which explain the judgment.

A second consideration also leads to the verdict of 'not proven'. The 'statistical fallacy' is notorious. In his famous study of suicide, Emile Durkheim worked with statistics: people are more likely to kill themselves in a Protestant than a Catholic country, in a cold country than in a warm country. What we cannot suppose is that in any particular case these factors are relevant. So if a housemaid in nineteenth-century Stockholm kills herself one winter, it does not follow that *her* suicide had anything to do with religion or temperature. In such a case it would be obviously invalid to infer that she killed herself because of the temperature and the religion, no matter what the statistics.

Above all it is statistics which *seem* to endorse the explaining away tactics. If 82% of people who like Corot have been to university (an invented statistic) or earn more than the national average wage, this does nothing at all to show that these factors explain the liking: this would lead us to the absurd conclusion that Mr X likes Corot *because he has a certain income*. The 'explaining away' manoeuvre gets much of its apparent 'obviousness' on the basis of irrelevant statistics.

We stand in this position: nothing has been shown to the effect that it is impossible that a value judgment should be justified and right, but neither has anything been said as to how such a justification would proceed. It is to that that we now turn.

3. Elizabeth David and evaluations

There is an idealisation of the process of genuine explanation. It is supposed that an explanation of the value of a picture would be complete and foolproof: something like the explanation why the internal angles of a triangle add up to one hundred and eighty degrees. But it is obvious that there could be no such proof that a painting is good.

The reasons for valuing a picture as a work of art are never going to be compelling in that way. From this has been drawn the hasty conclusion that there can be no reason given in support of judgments about the excellence or otherwise of paintings.

Thinking has long been indebted to eating: we digest ideas, chew things over; we roast or make mincemeat of our opponents, while students are grilled; books can be rotten or bland and are sometimes spicy. It is not surprising, then, if those who know most about food should have something to teach us about how to do philosophy. Philosophy's debt to Elizabeth David – who over many years has informed and inspired the regeneration of cooking and eating in this country – has not yet been properly acknowledged.

At some imprecise moment it dawned on Elizabeth David that the food she ate in France in the 1950s was far finer than the food she ate at that time in England; but how is this value judgment – not in itself a startling one – to be justified? Had she canvassed the prevailing strategies for justification, she might have made a list of the following:

1. French cooking is better just because I think so.
2. It is more rational to like French food.
3. God has revealed that it is in his divine plan that humans should prefer French to English cuisine.
4. French cooking is better for our health (it is 'biologically more efficient').
5. It is a 'scientifically verifiable fact' that French food is finer than English.

None of these strategies is very plausible, however; and we find ourselves in a similar position when it comes to justifying judgments about the quality of works of art. The inspiration Mrs David provides is in the way she proceeds to justify her judgment: she writes a five-hundred page book, *French Provincial Cooking*. But why did it take her five hundred pages to justify a single-sentence judgment?

A number of strategies are pursued at once: we are given insight into how the cooking proceeds and explanation of the point of various procedures, then our sense of taste has the opportunity of develop by seeing the relation of ancestry and cousinhood between dishes, learning to taste refinements and purity, we find ourselves at home in a complex network of practices and traditions which come to make more and more sense as we think about them in different contexts: we see the relation between eating and health, but also between eating and conversation, between various practices and traditions of care and thrift and celebration. There does not emerge a single, primitive, basis for preference, rather lots and lots of little points are made, and this goes hand in hand with the development of a more discriminating and informed palate: none of which, perhaps, is decisive on its own, but cumulatively they approach justification. This might be called Venetian Justification. There is no solid ground upon which the city is built. But by way of millions of piers driven into the lagoon it does actually (still) stand, although no pier on its own can be thought of as uniquely supporting it. Our judgments of taste are like Venice: ultimately precarious, but nevertheless raising themselves beautifully above the water; there is no bedrock of justification to which they are attached, but the multiplicity of little supports allows us to approach security. Elizabeth David's five hundred pages are five hundred little piers all supporting the central judgment.

On this model a poor judgment is one which is supported by very few or flimsy piers. If a picture is extolled merely because it is provocative, then only one flimsy support sustains it. The judgment about the excellence of the Corot is sustained by many supports. But what exactly are the supports for a judgment about the quality of a painting? The body of this book has been taken up with the attempt to provide reasons of the appropriate kind.

4. A formal statement

In this final section I shall lay out, in more formal terms, the central issues relevant to deciding whether or not judgments of artistic merit can have inter-subjective validity. When a judgment has inter-subjective validity, it does not hold merely for the individual who judges the work in question, but for all who judge it. Thus, if the judgment '*Avignon from the West* [plate 1] is of high artistic value' is inter-subjectively valid, then whosoever assesses the work's merit accurately will agree with this judgment; should someone disagree, their judgment would be flawed. The question is whether judgments of artistic merit are valid in this way.[3]

Trying to *establish* that judgments of artistic merit are inter-subjectively valid (which hereafter I shall call the 'inter-subjective thesis', for ease of reference) is a complex task. In fact, I do not believe that it can be established in the face of determined scepticism. The following paragraphs aim at something less conclusive. The concern here is more with persuasion than with proof. Persuasion short of proof involves two basic tasks. The first is to provide some reasonable grounds for thinking that the proposition (the intersubjective thesis) is true. These grounds will not amount to a demonstration. Secondly, obstacles to the acceptance of the thesis have to be removed; this is the task which the later paragraphs of this section try to accomplish. Good work can be done in both these fields (reasonable support and removal of obstacles) short of demonstrating conclusively that the proposition is true. There are some very obvious judgments about artistic merit whose inter-subjective validity it would be odd to deny. Suppose someone holds that I am a better draughtsman than Raphael; the error of this judgment would seem to be more than a matter of opinion. It would be compelling to suggest that the judge did not understand what was meant by 'artistic value'. Perhaps he simply preferred my drawings or found them politically appealing. That is all very well, but these are not judgments of artistic value as understood in this book. Why might someone deny that 'Raphael is the better draughtsman' is inter-subjectively valid? Perhaps that person is *already convinced* that such judgments just cannot be valid in this way. But that is not a presupposition which can legitimately be brought in at this stage. It rests upon an objection to the thesis which will be discussed later.[4]

People can be mistaken about artistic value. There are three distinct cases of this which are widely acknowledged. The first is in respect of judgments about work from other cultures. I am ill equipped to judge the artistic merit of a Chinese painting. Although I can prefer one painting to another, I do not understand what is of importance to the artist, I cannot pick up on subtleties and emphases which require a grasp of the relevant tradition. Nor can I properly evaluate the values the pictures express. But to admit this is to admit the possibility of inter-subjectively valid judgments. In this case accurate assessment would differ from my judgment. My judgment in this case is flawed and incomplete; it is not too hard to see why. I am in a poor position to understand the work of art.[5]

A second way in which one can be mistaken about artistic merit arises in connection with aesthetic education, as discussed in Chapter 8. Most people – as their taste develops and changes – would admit that their judgment at some past time was flawed. Either they overestimated some favourite or they underestimated the merit of a work they have come to appreciate. In their self-conception, most people work with the idea that some judgments of artistic merit can be flawed or incomplete.

A third way in which mistakes occur is collective. The poor reception which the first Impressionist exhibition received is famous. Most spectators' judgment of the artistic merit of the pictures was flawed. Doubtless there were understandable reasons *why* it was hard for those spectators to appreciate those works. The manner of the painting was unfamiliar and opposed to well established norms, there was official opposition and there were press diatribes. But none of this takes away from the fact that their judgment was flawed. To grant this is to grant that there was an inter-subjectively valid judgment by comparison with which the popular judgment was flawed. This example shows, too, that we should not construe inter-subjective validity in terms of a simple consensus: a consensus judgment about artistic merit can be flawed.

In the discussion of appreciation in Chapter 1, emphasis was placed upon the reasons the spectator has for his evaluation of the artistic merit of a particular work. In Chapters 4 and 5 examples of appropriate reasons were perused in a fairly systematic way. Appropriate reasons for judging artistic value concern the exploitation of the resources of the art-form, the manner in which content has been formed, the importance of the content as formed. And such reasons have to be concerned with the works as intrinsically valuable and as irreplaceable objects of attention. Such reason-giving traces an individual's appreciation of a particular work. But to be relevant to appreciation, the reasons have to be couched in an a-personal way. That is, such reasons are cast without reference to the fact that it is I who am looking at the painting. The reasons presented for a judgment about the merit of Corot's *Avignon* in Chapter 1 bear this out. At a deep level the practice of appreciation presupposes that the reasons which support judgments of artistic merit are inter-subjectively valid. Another way of putting this is to point out that the practice of reason-giving (relevant to appreciation) can be understood as the attempt to give anyone grounds for judging the work in a certain way.

The practice of reason-giving makes a claim upon the spectator. Suppose someone gives a number of appropriate reasons in support of the judgment that a work is of high artistic merit. I cannot then turn round and reply simply: 'Well, I don't like it.' Or, rather, if I do I will be retreating from the level of discussion which is central to appreciation. If I need to counter reasons with reasons, it is because reasons have a claim upon my judgment. To accept this is to accept that the reasons which support judgments of artistic merit can be inter-subjectively valid. And this validity extends to the supported judgments themselves.

In the discussion of the achievements of painting in Chapter 5, mention was made of a special kind of content which some paintings have. Paintings by Velásquez and Chardin were understood as presenting the spectator with visual images of things not generally available to vision. In these cases it was the fugitive quality of youthful beauty and 'the tenderness of years' which were 'bodied forth to sense'.

These pictures make vividly present content which we ought to take seriously. That is, an inter-subjective claim is made concerning the importance of what these pictures offer us. Naturally, people disagree about what is important: what seems crucial to me seems trivial to you. But this disagreement concerns *which* inter-subjective claims are valid. The disagreement here is not about *whether* there can be inter-subjectively valid claims about what is important.

In so far as the artistic value of some works is intimately bound up with the importance of what they offer the spectator, judgments about artistic value share the former's possibility of inter-subjective validity.

There is a special kind of consensus about the artistic value of certain works, namely that which transcends differences of time and place. The passage from Longinus quoted above gives a perfect expression of this point. If a work sustains the judgment that it is of high artistic merit, and on similar grounds, across a wide range of judges, then this gives ground for thinking that the judgment is inter-subjectively valid, and that those who disagree with it have flawed judgment with respect to that work.

This special consensus does not establish that the judgment is inter-subjectively valid. Yet it supports the view that it is so valid. Nor does this point contravene one made earlier in connection with collective mistakes. The consensus against the Impressionists was not of the kind Longinus specifies – that is, one which records agreement across diverse places and times.

These considerations make a positive case for the *initial plausibility* of the inter-subjective thesis. But it is possible that one might reply: 'Yes, very well, you have shown that it is at first sight plausible to regard such judgments in this way. But all the same I have a couple of devastating objections up my sleeve. So much the worse for superficial plausibility.' In the passages which follow I seek to defuse some of the possible objections to the inter-subjective thesis.

It goes without saying that people disagree about matters of artistic merit. The mere fact of disagreement does nothing on its own to undermine the inter-subjective thesis. Many factual claims generate disagreements: why do some people and not others develop skin cancer? But this does not in any way tarnish the possibility of an inter-subjectively valid answer here. It just happens that compelling evidence cannot at this stage be brought to demonstrate which of the competing claims is inter-subjectively valid. This point is liable to push the under-lying issue, with respect to artistic merit, to the surface. What is special about judgments of artistic merit – and what shows that they cannot be inter-subjectively valid – is that there is no stable method for showing which of rival claims is correct. There is no reliable way of deciding whether any particular claim about artistic merit is inter-subjectively valid or not. The concern, then, is with the mode of demonstration.

There are methods of validation for judgments about artistic merit which have already been discussed. Critical practice can aim at such justification, and sustained con-sensus among connoisseurs gives good grounds for thinking that certain judgments of artistic merit are inter-subjectively valid. However, these methods of vali-dation remain defeasible. There are examples of apparent critical validation and consensus among connoisseurs which were mistaken. Vermeer, for example, was under-rated through the eighteenth and nineteenth centuries; Correggio, by contrast, was over-rated. But we ought to note that this revision is a matter of emphasis. Vermeer was never considered a useless painter, and although his reputation runs lower, critical and connoisseur consensus still rate Correggio as a fine painter.

Judgments of artistic merit do not lack methods of verification. However, this may not satisfy the sceptic. These processes of verification, in comparison with those of natural science, are vague and inconclusive. The claim, then, is that judgments about artistic value cannot be inter-subjectively valid because there is no *conclusive* method of verification. It is not clear, however, that for a judgment to be inter-subjectively valid there *must* be a conclusive method of validation.

A process of justification has to be suited to the kind of judgment it seeks to uphold. The fact that a process of validation cannot mirror those of the natural sciences does

not thereby discredit its pretensions to justification. What
we are seeking validation for (a judgment about artistic
value) is not a matter tractable in terms of natural science.
But it is an unsupported dogma to claim that only matters
tractable in terms of natural science can allow of inter-
subjectively valid claims. That is the dogma of *Scientism*.
And recognising this dogma for what it is has nothing to
do with discrediting the inter-subjective validity of scientific projects. The claim that natural science alone can
furnish us with inter-subjectively valid propositions is not
itself a claim which can be justified from within natural
science. Scientism is logically incoherent.

Still, supposing the sceptic reluctantly goes along with
this, there is ground for disagreement. 'The problem', they
say, 'with the modes of validation you have cited as appropriate to judgments about artistic value is that they are
based on feeling.' Suppose it is granted that the absence
of scientific demonstration does not necessarily rule out
inter-subjective validity. The problem lies with this particular purported validation.

The fact that judgments about artistic value depend
upon feeling is not disputed.[6] The question is whether this
must compromise the inter-subjective validity of such a
judgment. Is it possible that a judgment be *both* dependent upon feeling and inter-subjectively valid? To see that
it can be we need to think about the way in which we can
stand in judgment upon feelings – our own and those of
others. We can reproach someone, or ourselves, for being
cold or callous, we can praise warmheartedness, we can
judge a reaction as oversensitive, a fear as unfounded.
There is nothing about feelings as such which prevents
them from being judged, nor those judgments from being
inter-subjectively valid. If I judge that Charlotte gets
embarrassed too easily, I am making a judgment about
her feelings. The judgment purports to be inter-subjectively valid, and there is no reason why some judgments

of this kind should not be inter-subjectively valid. Judgments about artistic value incorporate this standing in judgment upon feelings. The judgment that Corot's *Avignon* is a work of great artistic stature depends in part upon a felt reaction to the work. It is quite possible that some other spectator will not have such a felt response: the work will leave them cold, as it were. But this does not show that there is a problem with the inter-subjective validity of the judgment about artistic value. For one can judge that certain spectators are inadequately sensitive to certain qualities of the work. And we are not in general averse to the thought that there can be inter-subjectively valid judgment about feelings.

It goes without saying that we might be in disagreement about which feelings a spectator ought to have, or about which feelings are called for by a work. But as has already been pointed out, disagreement does not show that there cannot be inter-subjectively valid judgments: it only makes it evident that which claims are so valid is not always obvious.

It is crucial to note that a judgment can be inter-subjectively valid and yet not very important. Personally, I do not think that it matters very much whether someone does or does not appreciate Corot's *Avignon*. The inter-subjectively valid claim that it is a fine work is not a way of trying to bully the preferences of others, namely those preferences which run counter to the inter-subjectively valid judgment – for example, someone who finds *Avignon* tedious. I think that sometimes people shy away from the inter-subjective thesis because of a moral scruple; the scruple is that they would seem to be domineering and directive of others.

In fact, we have to distinguish between two importantly different questions. The first question is: Can judgments of artistic merit be inter-subjectively valid? The second question is: Is it important that one's preferences coincide with inter-subjectively valid judgments about artistic merit? How bad is it if one likes works which are not all that good from the point of view of artistic value? One could be absolutely adamant that the answer to the first question is 'yes' while giving a very cautious answer to the second. It may not, in terms of the goodness of a person's life, matter very much whether his preferences in respect of painting display much sensitivity to genuine artistic merit. Or it may. In any case, the answer to the second question is not dictated by espousal of the inter-subjective thesis. Thus the scruple does not really present an obstacle to the acceptance of that thesis.

In this section I have not established the inter-subjective thesis. However, I hope to have provided enough evidence for two weaker but still important conclusions. First, it is not *obvious* that judgments about artistic merit can only ever have validity for oneself (the person who makes the judgment). We are not entitled to take that position for granted. Secondly, it is entirely respectable, from an intellectual point of view, to hold to the inter-subjective thesis.

The intellectual high ground apart, the inter-subjective thesis can sometimes seem to be psychologically compromised. It is true that some people maintain an absolutism about artistic value in a way which says a lot about them and little about artistic value. It betrays their need for an absolute and their determination to see themselves as servants or champions of that absolute. In the face of this pathology, it can look as if it is more mature, more sane, to prescind from inter-subjective statements about artistic value.

But this opposition of psychological states – the tense, brittle absolutism *versus* the relaxed, friendly, 'each to his own' attitude – this opposition is not the whole truth. We have already seen how the inter-subjective thesis is *not* the claim that people should be made to fall into line with an inter-subjectively valid judgment about artistic value. It is not a bully's licence. The pathology of absolutism adheres to the second issue and does not compromise the inter-subjective thesis itself.

Further, the embracing of 'each to his own' or 'who am I to judge' views *can* in its way also be a pathology. It can represent the flight from authority and a refusal maturely to recognise oneself as a possible source of authority. It can represent cowardice, the flight from frightening disputes.

The psychological high ground belongs to neither side.

Notes

1. Herodotus, *Histories*, Book 2, section 47.

2. Longinus, *On the Sublime*, section viii.

3. I shall discuss inter-subjective validity rather than objectivity. The word 'objective' is used in so many different ways that it tends to breed confusion. Sometimes, 'objective' is used merely as a synonym for 'inter-subjectively valid'. Sometimes, it is used to characterise *properties* which an object has apart from human perception, for example extension and weight. I do not want to get entangled in the debate about whether artistic merit (which is a value) can be objective in the latter sense.

4. This is not to rule out – of course – that most judgments about artistic merit are much less clear cut than this example. The judgment that *Avignon* is Corot's finest painting is neither obviously right nor obviously wrong. But the claim before us is only that *some* judgments about artistic merit command inter-subjective validity.

5. Note that I might think that the work is very fine and a connoisseur also think that it is very fine and my judgment still be flawed in that I do not hold it for the right reasons.

6. This is not to say that they are based on feeling *alone*.

A Note on Further Reading

Rather than try to provide a bibliography let me just mention some books which I have found helpful in thinking about painting. This list is entirely personal and in no sense a fair assessment of the field. The books do not all relate to painting directly, but provide food for thought. A date given in brackets is the date of original publication, or of writing in the case of Schiller. The date of the edition cited may seem alarmingly distant, but, generally, the works mentioned are available in much more recent impressions.

Clarke, Kenneth, *Landscape into Art*, London: John Murray, 1949.

Pater, Walter, *The Renaissance* (1873).

Proust, Marcel, 'Chardin' in *Contre Sainte-Beuve, suivi de Nouveaux Mélanges*, Paris: Pléiade, 1954.

Remembrance of Things Past (1913-1927), trans. Scott Moncrieff and Kilmartin, Harmondsworth: Penguin, 1983.

Schiller, Friedrich, *Letters on the Aesthetic Education of Man* (1793), trans. Wilkinson and Willoughby, Oxford: Clarendon Press, 1967.

Scruton, Roger, *The Aesthetics of Architecture*, London: Methuen & Co., 1979.

Stokes, Adrian, *Stones of Rimini*, London, 1934.

Wölfflin, Heinrich, *Classic Art* (1898), trans. Murray and Murray, Oxford: Phaidon, 1952.

Works of a purer philosophical strain make special demands upon the reader, but sometimes yield the richer fruit.

G.F.W. Hegel, Introduction to *Lectures on Aesthetics* (1835), trans. Knox, London, 1975.
Kant, Immanuel, *Critique of Judgment* (1790), trans. Meredith, Oxford: Clarendon Press, 1964
Budd, Malcolm, *Values of Art*, London, 1995.
Mothersill, Mary, *Beauty Restored*, Oxford: Clarendon Press, 1984.
Wollheim, Richard, *Painting as an Art*, London: Thames and Hudson, 1987.

Index